Conquer Your Motivation

First Printed in Great Britain by
Obex Publishing Ltd in 2020

2 4 6 8 10 9 7 5 3 1

Copyright Jean-Claude Leveque, 2020

Jean-Claude Leveque has asserted his right under
the Copyright, Designs and Patents Act 1988 to be
identified as the author of this work.

All rights reserved. No parts of this publication may
be reproduced, stored in a retrieval system, or
transmitted in any form or by any means, electronic,
mechanical, photocopying, recording or otherwise,
without the prior permission of the copyright
owner.

Paperback ISBN	978-1-913454-09-8
eBook ISBN	978-1-913454-10-4

A CIP catalogue record for this book is available
from the British Library.

Obex Publishing Ltd.
Reg. No. 12169917

CONTENTS

CHAPTER 1: WHAT IS MOTIVATION? 10

    INTRINSIC AND EXTRINSIC MOTIVATION 14
    ENJOY THE SNOWBALL EFFECT 17
    THE BENEFITS OF MOTIVATION 19
    THE DANGERS OF A LACK OF MOTIVATION 21
    POINTS TO REMEMBER FROM THIS CHAPTER 23

CHAPTER 2: THE DANGERS OF PROCRASTINATION 25

    HOW DOES PROCRASTINATION AFFECT YOUR LIFE? 28
    THE MILESTONE TECHNIQUE 32
    WHAT WILL IT FEEL LIKE TOMORROW? 34
    POINTS TO REMEMBER FROM THIS CHAPTER 36

CHAPTER 3: ARE YOU MOTIVATED? 38

    ASK SOMEONE ELSE'S OPINION 43
    ACKNOWLEDGE YOUR NEED TO CHANGE AND COMMIT TO IT 44
    POINTS TO REMEMBER FROM THIS CHAPTER 46

CHAPTER 4: START WITH AN EVEN FOUNDATION 48

    PHYSICAL AND MENTAL DECLUTTERING FOR EXTRA MOTIVATION 49
    LIFESTYLE CHANGES FOR EXTRA DAILY FOCUS 55
    POINTS TO REMEMBER FROM THIS CHAPTER 63

CHAPTER 5: THE IMPORTANCE OF EFFECTIVE TIME MANAGEMENT 64

    HOW DOES TIME MANAGEMENT INCREASE MOTIVATION? 67
    5 TIME MANAGEMENT TECHNIQUES TO TRY 71
    IT'S OKAY TO SAY "NO" SOMETIMES 83
    WHY GOAL SETTING IS VITAL FOR INCREASED MOTIVATION 86
    POINTS TO REMEMBER FROM THIS CHAPTER 88

CHAPTER 6: 15 STRATEGIES TO NATURALLY BOOST YOUR

MOTIVATION **90**

    VISUALISE THE END GOAL 94
    HAVE A LONG TERM PLAN 99
    ASSESS WHAT IS MOTIVATING YOU 103
    USE DELAYED GRATIFICATION METHODS 107
    FIGURE OUT YOUR MOST PRODUCTIVE TIME OF DAY 113
    USE TIME CHALLENGES 118
    DEVELOP A POSITIVE MINDSET 123
    SET DAILY AND WEEKLY GOALS 132
    CELEBRATE YOUR SUCCESSES 137
    USE SCHEDULING 142
    EAT THE FROG (NOT LITERALLY!) 147
    AVOID OVERTHINKING 152
    IDENTIFY YOUR PERSONAL MENTAL BLOCKS AND OVERCOME THEM 158
    HAVE A QUICK WORKOUT 163
    BRIBE YOURSELF WITH A CONTRACT 167
    POINTS TO REMEMBER FROM THIS CHAPTER 171

CONCLUSION **173**

    WHERE TO BEGIN 175

Introduction

How did you feel when you wake up this morning? Think back to this morning and try and remember how you felt when your alarm went off, and you knew that you had to open your eyes and get ready to take on the world once more.

Did you wake up and feel energised, ready to face the day ahead? Did you feel like you wanted an extra five minutes in bed, but you were keen to get on with your tasks for the day? Or, did you wake up feeling like you simply didn't want to get out of bed at all and you snoozed your alarm five times before finally admitting defeating and getting up?

All too many of us fall into that final category. If that's you, don't worry, you're in good company!

It's not that we're lazy, it's simply that we lack the motivation to do the things we need to do. Why? Because they're not interesting to us and we don't know how to make them interesting or to manipulate our own minds into getting them done anyway. These things are items we need to do, things that don't really hold much excitement or reward, but we have no choice. There are bound to be many of these things in your life, and you're likely to procrastinate on many of them too.

Again, don't worry, you're in good company!

It's not easy to be motivated by something which you don't care about, and something which isn't going to benefit you in any way. However, there are tasks in our lives that are important despite the lack of interest or the lack of direct benefit to you - if you're tasked with doing something at work, that means your job relies upon you actually finding the motivation to get it done. If you have to do something in your personal life, despite the fact it makes you yawn with boredom, ticking it off your list is a must-do.

The problem is, if we lack motivation, then we automatically lack productivity. In a working situation especially, a lack of motivation can be a huge problem. Even in your personal life, having no motivation basically means that you're going to do literally nothing. You'll sit there, wasting your day and before you know it, it's nighttime again and you've no idea where the day went. Over a lifetime, a lack of motivation adds up to regret and opportunities lost.

When you think about it, a lack of motivation basically means you're wasting your life in some way. Is that something you want? Do you want to look back in 30 or 40 years' time and think 'damn! Why didn't I just go for it?' Regrets can eat away at you if you let them, but choosing not to develop them in the first place is the best way forward. That all starts with a little motivation.

Your life doesn't have to be that way; you don't have to look back and wish you'd done more. This book is going to change your perception of motivation, help you boost your own natural motivation levels, and find a way to grab your "get up and go" once more. If yours is constantly running away from you, slipping away before you have a chance to rein it in when you open your eyes, this book will be your personal plan on how to harness it, capture it, keep it, and use it.

Sure, there will always be days when you wish you could stay in bed and do nothing but watch Netflix and literally chill the hell out, but by understanding the ins and outs of motivation and knowing how to increase yours, these days will become less frequent and as a result, far less damaging to your day and your overall health and wellbeing. We all love a lazy day and sometimes they're necessary, but when it happens every day, you need to make a change - fast.

Is it possible to be healthy when you lack motivation? Not really. If you lack the will to do things, that basically means you're either low in mood or you're simply not focusing on your health and the goals you have in life. Neither situation is a good one. At best, you'll end up with regrets; at worst, you'll end up extremely unhappy and unhealthy.

So, have a quiet word with yourself. Ask yourself whether or not you have the right amount of motivation in your life. If not, don't panic, you simply need to read this book and get started on your own personal journey towards ultra motivation in your life. We're going to help you, and by the end, you should be feeling the first bubbles of excitement for your new road ahead.

It all starts with just one step!

Chapter 1:
What is Motivation?

When you hear a word, any word, you usually automatically think you know what it means, but if someone asks you to define it clearly, you struggle. It's a sense of knowing something but not having the words for it.

Motivation is one of those words. Confidence is another. These are words which are very commonly used, and when someone says the word you nod knowingly because of course, you know what motivation and confidence are, but if someone says to you 'okay, define it for me', you're left umming and ahhing, without the words to use.

You see, motivation cannot be seen or measured, it cannot be touched, tasted or smelled, but it can certainly be felt.

Perhaps that's why there is such a mystery around motivation. When we can't see something with our eyes or measure it in real terms, we tend to become fearful or questioning. We like things we can see, and this is why scientists and researchers have long been confused about motivation. They doubt it and worry about it because there is no way to harness it physically. However, there are many ways you can harness it mentally and use it for your own good.

So, how can we define this magical word?

Motivation is a feeling. It is a sense of urgency, of wanting to do something and being pushed to do it. However, the forces that are doing the pushing are completely internal.

Motivation has both a subjective and objective element too. You can be motivated to do something because you want to, you need to, or because it's going to bring you gains, or you can be motivated not to do something, e.g. to run away from something (a possible punishment or a desire to simply not do a particular task) or hide something.

In terms of this book, we're going to focus on the type of motivation that pushes you to achieve. There's no good in trying to run away from things or trying to stop things from happening. What will be, will be. We're focusing on the productive, the positive, and that means trying to increase your motivation in life, in order to achieve the things you want to achieve and get all the items on your to-do list ticked off. This type of motivation also helps you to grow as a person, as it increases your confidence levels and allows you to hit large life goals that could even change the course of your life altogether. Everything starts with an action, and that action needs motivation in order to make it a reality from the get-go.

Of course, motivation ebbs and flows. You might wake up on 1 January and be very motivated to go to the gym. You want to work off all those festive season pounds and you're focused on feeling your fittest and healthiest in a short space of time. However, after a week or two of going to the gym, you might find that your motivation drops a little, and as a result, you might find yourself skipping gym sessions. By the time the middle of February rolls around, you realise that you've been going to the gym less and less, simply because your motivation has gone back to bed until 1 January once more.

The key is to find a way to trigger the initial motivation and then keep it going, learning ways in which to kickstart a motivation boost whenever needed. It's also about finding the initial motivation when it's hard to do so, e.g. when there's something you need to complete but the entire thing is boring and not at all inspiring to you. Life is about the enjoyable things and the not so enjoyable things, but both are equally as important.

In order to be able to kickstart motivation, you first need to learn about the ins and outs of this very subject. Knowing the background knowledge helps you to understand and when you understand something, you're better placed to achieve it. So, let's now focus on the main types of motivation - intrinsic and extrinsic, and learn more about what they mean and how they're useful to you.

Intrinsic And Extrinsic Motivation

When you start reading up on motivation, you'll quickly come across two different types, namely intrinsic motivation and extrinsic motivation. This basically refers to the thing you're motivated by, and that has an effect on how you can boost your motivation in the future.

- **Intrinsic motivation** - If you're intrinsically motivated you're motivated by your own desire to do something for you. For instance, you might be motivated to learn a new language simply because you want to and you enjoy it or going swimming because you feel less stressed afterwards. Generally speaking, there is no reward attached to intrinsic motivation; it is purely because it's something you enjoy or because doing it helps you feel better in yourself.
- **Extrinsic motivation** - If you're extrinsically motivated then you're motivated by a factor outside of yourself, e.g. a reward or trying to avoid an outcome you don't want. If you're motivated by money, you're extrinsically motivated. Other examples are perhaps reading a textbook because you need to study for an exam, or doing a full

clean of your house because you've got the in-laws coming around.

You might think that the type of motivation doesn't matter, as long as there is some kind of motivation to give you a kick and get you going, but being motivated by the wrong things can sometimes be as bad as not being motivated at all. You need to focus on the positives in life in order to generate more positives your way. If you focus on negatives, they will be followed by more negatives. It's not rocket science.

When you first read about the types of motivation above, you might automatically think that it's always better to be intrinsically motivated than extrinsically, but that's not always the case, and it really depends upon the situation at hand. Provided the reason for your motivation is healthy, that's when it doesn't really matter. Extrinsic motivation can actually be a very good booster to get going or to keep going when the going is tough.

We're often extrinsically motivated more than we are intrinsical, e.g. we are pre-programmed to look for a reward or a compliment. You shouldn't beat yourself up internally for that, because it's part and parcel of being human, but you should try and examine your reasons for doing things and find a healthier reason if you can. For instance, it's better to be motivated to learn to swim because you want to become healthier, and not for the reason that you don't want people to laugh at the fact you can't swim yet. It's about changing your mindset and looking at your reasons why.

As you learn to motivate yourself, using the techniques throughout this book, you will automatically learn to look for positive ways to motivate yourself, rather than negative ones. Overall, both extrinsic and intrinsic methods are useful at different times and provided you're working towards a positive outcome, without any bad feeling or trying to avoid something, you're on a healthy road forwards anyway.

Enjoy The Snowball Effect

The good news is that once you start to use motivational techniques, you'll find that your sense of motivation increases quite quickly, along with your happiness, your mood, your confidence, and your general sense of what is possible in life. The more you do, the more you want, and the more you realise is out there waiting for you. It's a wonderful feeling as it grows within you, and more opportunities come your way as a result.

It's a little like a snowball on the edge of a hill. At first, the ball is very small and isn't useful for anything, but the more snow you add to it, the bigger it becomes. As it becomes bigger, it becomes heavier and it gains strength. When it's big enough, it starts to roll and the more momentum it builds up, the faster it moves. It picks up more and more snow as it rolls down the hill, and before you know it, it becomes an unstoppable force that nothing and nobody can challenge.

Your motivation can do the same if you dedicate the time and effort to making it work for you. Some methods will give you a high feeling quite quickly and it will spur you on to do more. Then, as you achieve small milestones, you'll feel even more motivated, and the story continues. However, it might be that other methods give you a slow burn effect; you don't notice much happening straight away, but over time the gains are huge. It's only when you look back and see what you achieved, that you realise the methods worked wonderfully well to keep you on track and to stop you from giving in when things got a little tough.

So, the best advice is to stick with it. Try different techniques and see how you feel after a while. Motivation in any guise, provided it's towards the right things and for the right reason, is never a bad aim to have!

The Benefits of Motivation

Of course, being motivated is better than not being motivated, but why exactly? What does it do for us and why do we need it? Why can't we just get on with things without needing a push to do it? Because we're human, basically.

Again, it's one of those things that we automatically assume we know, but when we're asked to define it, we can't!

So, what are the benefits of increased motivation exactly?

- **Improved mood** - When you feel uplifted, it has a direct impact on your mood overall. You feel uplifted, it gives you purpose, and you're more likely to surge forward and complete the task as a result. Of course, feeing uplifted and happy is a far healthier way to live and a more pleasant one too.
- **Gives you something to aim for** - When you're motivated, you're trying to achieve something and that means you have something to aim for. Having goals to aim for ensures that you're not

wasting your time on things that don't matter or even on unhealthy habits.
- **Helps to create opportunities** - Motivation means you're pushing forward and you're doing, and when you do that you're automatically encouraging doors to open. It's like a chain reaction; the more you do, the more the doors open and the more chances and opportunities come your way. Of course, it's up to you which opportunities you take and which you don't, but they're there to decide between at the very least.
- **Forges a positive mindset** - A happier mood and more opportunities help to boost a positive mindset and when you're more positive. Positivity is a healthy route towards positive mental and physical health.
- **Beneficial for your work** - Being motivated in your work is very impressive to your manager and that could be beneficial for your future career prospects.
- **Helps you get more done during the day** - Of course, when you're motivated you're doing more and that means you have greater control over your to-do list. You're more productive overall and you're more able to hit targets and deadlines in both your personal and professional lives.

- **Reduced stress** - Being in control of your work and the tasks you need to do generally helps to reduce stress, which is very beneficial for health and wellbeing overall.

The Dangers of a Lack of Motivation

To complete the picture, let's look at what a lack of motivation can do to your life and your future prospects.

It's important to get into the crux of the matter and try and work out why you're not motivated. Are you simply not motivated to do one task? Are you not motivated in general? How do you feel?

Lack of motivation is a symptom of depression, but if you're not motivated that doesn't automatically mean that you're depressed. However, if your lack of motivation is associated with low mood and other depression symptoms, that's something you need to address first and foremost. In this case, reach out to those around you, get help and support and see your doctor. There are many treatment routes for depression these days and nobody needs to live with the condition. There's no shame in reaching out either - it's true strength!

Assuming that there isn't a deeper reason behind your lack of motivation, it's simply not a good headspace to be in. You will feel low, you will feel lacking in confidence, and you'll feel more stressed as a result of a mounting to-do list. Again, this isn't healthy.

Overall, you're not productive. You're not hitting your headlines, you're not reaching your targets, and your manager at work might start to notice.

The dangers of a lack of motivation are the direct opposite of all the wonderful benefits we've just mentioned. Doors won't open because you're not doing anything to try and open them. Your health will be affected because you're more likely to be stressed and overwhelmed with everything you need to do. You won't be as productive and you're probably going to have a negative mindset in general.

It's not a pleasant picture.

Points to Remember From This Chapter

This chapter has introduced the definition of motivation and looked into the different types, while also talking about why it's good to be motivated and bad not to be.

As we mentioned, motivation is one of those words that everyone assumes they know about, but when you ask them to put a definition on it, it's hard to do. You can't increase the presence of something in your life if you don't know what it is!

The main points to take from this chapter are:

- Motivation is an inner desire to do something or to avoid something
- Motivation cannot be seen or measured, but it can be felt
- There are two main types of motivation - intrinsic and extrinsic and they can both be beneficial in different ways
- Identifying your reasons for wanting to do something, e.g. your reason for motivation ensures that you're doing things for the right reasons, and

not in order to avoid something or impress someone else
- Being motivated helps increase general health and wellbeing, as well as productivity
- A lack of motivation can be a sign of depression when accompanied by other symptoms
- Motivation can help you to achieve more and create opportunities for future growth.

Chapter 2:
The Dangers of Procrastination

Motivation will quickly come to a full stop and dead-end when one particular issue becomes a frequent entity in your life.

We are of course talking about procrastination, the number one motivation killer known to man!

Procrastination will take a day full of productive promise, twist it around and cause you to achieve literally zero as a result. Of course, procrastination can be avoided and it can be managed, but you first have to understand what it is and unpick your reasons for actually procrastinating in the first place!

So, what exactly is procrastination?

Procrastination is the process of taking a task and basically putting it off until another time, usually until the next day. You do this because the task is either boring, uninspiring, or it's something that you're not sure how to do, or a task that seems too large to tackle.

As a result, your motivation to actually get started is zapped away before it's even had a chance to take hold.

Let's talk you through a couple of examples of procrastination, so you can identify whether this is a mainstay in your life too.

You're given a job at work, and you fully intend to get started on it, but when you start looking into what it entails, it seems huge. Not only do you need to research a subject, but you also need to pull that research together, put it into some kind of understandable format, write a report, and submit it. It seems like your own personal Everest and you simply don't know where to begin.

So, instead of looking for a suitable starting point and just throwing yourself into it, you think 'oh I'll start that tomorrow' and instead you focus on smaller tasks that have been sitting on your desk for a few days. You tell yourself that these smaller tasks are going to start becoming urgent if you don't do them soon, and by completing these five tasks you can tick five things off your to-do list, rather than no ticks as you start making progress on a large task that will take you several days.

Another example is a task that you simply don't like. Perhaps it's boring, perhaps it's time-consuming, but whatever the reason, you simply don't like it. Perhaps it's filing. Maybe it's ironing, it might even be going into town and sorting out your car insurance.

Whatever the task, it's not one that you find exciting or inspiring, so instead of just doing it and getting it over and done with, you tell yourself that you'll do it tomorrow. Then the next day, you tell yourself it'll be fine for another day. Before you know it, you've put that task for off a week.

Both of these are very common examples of procrastinating.

Now, if you're guilty of procrastinating, don't worry; we all do it so it doesn't make you an unmotivated, unproductive person, but it does mean that you need to work out how to kick this habit out of your life as much as possible.

To give you a reason to do that, let's look at why procrastination affects your life in a negative way.

How Does Procrastination Affect Your Life?

By procrastinating, you'll feel good at that specific moment in time. For instance, if you've been dreading doing a particular task and then you decide that you'll put it off until the next day, you might even get a small high from it. You don't have to do it today, you can do something more fun or generally more enjoyable.

However, that feeling won't last. The next day you'll wake up and realise that you need to do the task you put off yesterday. You might decide to procrastinate once more, or you might actually do it, but find yourself feeling under pressure because the job is now more urgent than it was yesterday. As a result, you start to feel stressed, and stress is not a healthy or welcome visitor in anyone's life.

The more you procrastinate, the more problems you cause yourself.

Putting off a task at work because it's boring or you can't figure out where to begin means that it's going to increase in urgency as the days tick by. The deadline for that task will then start to loom and you'll have to work every hour sent to you in order to get close to finishing it. You might even miss your deadline as a result of putting it off.

As jobs become more urgent, they stick in your mind. They're a constant nagging, a doubt in the back of your mind, pulling your mood down and causing you to worry more. Again, none of this makes for a happy life, and none of it makes for a healthy life either.

Procrastination causes stress over time, and stress is a potential killer over the long-term.

Of course, that doesn't mean that if you become a little stressed because you procrastinated for a few days, that doesn't mean that your health is about to take a serious downturn in fortunes, but if you continue to do this time and time again and your stress builds up over the long-term to dangerous levels, your entire health and wellbeing picture is affected to a very negative degree.

Put simply, constant procrastination puts pressure on you, it causes you to panic, it might cause anxiety and stress, and it makes small problems become huge mountainous problems, simply because you didn't complete a task at the first asking and instead put it off for a series of days.

You also run the risk of forgetting something if you procrastinate. That task that you didn't want to do for whatever reason, you might forget all about it. Then, when your manager comes to you and asks where the report is, or whatever else it entailed, you're dumbfounded and stuck to the spot, because you completely forgot about it. That doesn't make you look very productive or organised, and doesn't paint you in a good light.

The same can be said for any situation, it doesn't always have to be about work. It might be a study deadline you missed or a task at home that you've put off and now it's seriously overdue. Maybe you forgot to file your taxes because the thought of sitting down with a calculator and working everything out, pulling out all your records and filing in the form, just seemed too difficult at that moment in time. As a result, you're now looking at a letter from the tax office telling you that you're overdue on your tax return and you have to pay a fine and file it right now.

It causes panic, it causes stress, and in that situation, it costs you money too.

So, as you can see, procrastination is not something you need to invite into your life, and it's something you should be actively working on kicking out instead.

To overcome a procrastination habit, you first need to acknowledge that you're procrastinating in the first place. You might not actually realise you're doing it! So, when you put something off, ask yourself what you're doing, actually say to yourself "am I procrastinating here?" If the answer is yes, you can use the following two techniques to overcome the moment, find motivation, and actually get on with the task at hand.

The Milestone Technique

This particular technique is ideal to find the motivation to complete large tasks.

When you're giving a task that is going to take several days to complete, it's not as attractive as completing a smaller task. When you complete a smaller task or several smaller tasks, you're able to tick that item off your to-do list and get that 'competed' high quickly. It makes you feel like you've achieved something and not simply wasted your day.

However, when you're handed a large task, you're not going to be able to tick that item off your list for at least a few days, and it's going to eat up time every day until then. It's had to find the motivation when you're not getting a reward, e.g. the 'competed' high.

One way to find the motivation to get started on that ask and actually work on it until completion, without procrastinating, is to use the milestone technique.

When you feel the urge to put a large task off, acknowledge that you are indeed procrastinating. Tell yourself that you're falling foul of your procrastination habit simply because the task seems too large in the moment.

Then, look at the task and break it down into smaller milestones.

By doing this, you're taking the focus from completing a large task that is going to take several days before you get that wonderful feeling of completion and you're giving yourself smaller targets to meet. With every milestone you complete, you'll feel like you're making progress towards your final aim, and you're able to get that 'completed' high we just mentioned with every tick on one of your milestones.

Your motivation will increase every time you complete a smaller milestone, willing you on to complete the next one, then the next one, and finally, complete the entire task.

The feeling of actually completing a large task is fantastic, but finding the motivation to not only get started but keep going when a task takes a long time can be difficult. The milestone method can help you find that motivation and therefore make steady progress to the final stage.

What Will it Feel Like Tomorrow?

Another useful technique to overcome procrastination is to ask yourself what it will feel like tomorrow if you put this task off.

We tend to procrastinate on tasks that we don't want to do because they're boring or we're not sure how to get started, but that feeling is to going to go away. You will still need to do the task, whether it's today, tomorrow or the following day. So, the next time you're considering putting a task off and doing something different, usually something more interesting or fun, stop for a second and ask yourself how you'll feel tomorrow.

Will you be more stressed tomorrow because not only do you need to complete the task you're putting off, but you also need to work on other tasks too? Probably. Try and imagine how you're going to feel, how stressed you'll be, and how you probably won't manage to tick all the items off tomorrow's to-do list.

It's important to be realistic when using this tactic because its easy just to think 'oh, I'll manage it', but the chances are that by piling extra pressure onto the following day, you're simply setting yourself up for failure.

Once you've pictured how the following day is going to feel, vow to take some of the pressure off by simply getting on with the task right now. You could even promise yourself a reward at the end of the day when you've safely completed the task that's causing you so much annoyance.

Points to Remember From This Chapter

Procrastination is a serious productivity killer, and it's one which can easily side-track your day and ruin the following ones too. By procrastinating on a regular basis, you're actually increasing your stress levels, because those tasks aren't simply going to go away, they're just going to increase in urgency, until they start to force themselves onto your to-do list, regardless of what else you need to do.

The main points to take from this chapter are:

- Procrastination is something you need to try and kick out of your life as much as possible
- Many people don't realise they're procrastinating, so it's vital to become more aware of your actions and acknowledge when you're thinking about procrastinating on a specific task
- We often procrastinate when a task is too large, too boring, it's something we don't enjoy, or we're not sure how to do it
- Procrastination can increase stress levels and can also increase the risk of you forgetting specific tasks

- Stress will increase as takes become more urgent, the more you procrastinate on them
- Two useful anti-procrastination techniques are cutting large tasks down into achievable daily milestones, and imagining what the next day will be like if you put the task off.

Chapter 3:
Are You Motivated?

In order to figure out how much work you need to do on your motivation, you need to find out what your current motivation level is.

Now, as we mentioned earlier, it's very difficult to measure motivation because it's not something we can actually see or experience with any of our senses, other than a general feeling. For that reason, trying to figure out how motivated you are can be difficult.

It might also be that you're more motivated in some areas of your life compared to others. You might be very motivated in your personal life, but not so motivated in your working life, or maybe vice versa. You might even be motivated on certain tasks, but not on others.

The only way to really work out whether you're motivated or not, or whether you need to do a little work on your motivation levels, is to sit down and be honest with yourself.

This chapter is going to help you try and work out how motivated you are in general, but it's important to remember that motivation levels can ebb and flow throughout our lives. You might be ready and raring to go one minute, and then you might catch a cold or have a late-night, be feeling a little sluggish, and your motivation goes out of the window with it.

Motivation is very rarely ever-present, but we can find ways to try and increase its presence in our lives and look for ways to activate it again when it seems to have gone missing.

First things first, however, you need to find your own starting position.

Your Personal Motivation Assessment

Doing a quick motivation assessment will give you important information on the areas of your life where you're quite motivated and those where you could do with focusing a little more.

It's very unlikely that you're totally unmotivated. Most people have trouble spots when it comes to motivation; for instance, you might find it hard to motivate yourself on a Monday morning and as a result, the first day of your working week is normal pretty unproductive. You might find that you're a little unmotivated when it comes to general fitness because you're not a fan of the gym. Understanding the problem areas for you as an individual means you can put the measures in place to try and rectify the situation, or at least improve it.

Remember, nobody is perfect, and that means nobody can be super-motivated all the time.

So, grab a pen and paper and sit down somewhere comfortable. It's best if you can find a time when you're to going to be disturbed, so you can really focus your attention on working out your motivation starting point.

On your paper, write down seven different categories:

- Work
- Health
- Exercise
- Personal goals
- Personal life
- Personal development
- Career growth

Look at each one in turn and try and analyse your motivation level. For each one, try and identify problems that you have and scribble them down. At this point, your paper is just a brainstorming session, it doesn't have to be neat and tidy, so make sure you scribble whatever comes into your mind.

For instance, in the work section, do you struggle at certain times of the week? Do you have problems at a certain time of the day? Do you find certain types of tasks are harder to motivate yourself to do?

Be honest and open with yourself, as that's the only way to really make progress and work towards improving the current situation. Nobody else has to read this paper, and if you want to burn it afterwards to make sure, go for it! You simply need to feel free enough to write down everything pertinent that comes to your mind.

For the health section, do you find yourself falling into unhealthy habits quite easily because it seems easier, or are you motivated to make sure you eat a healthy diet, that you drink enough water every day?

Focus on each category and try and identify problems, analysing them as much as possible.

Once you have all the information to hand, you can identify areas to work on. It's a good idea to work on one at a time; otherwise, you might run the risk of overloading yourself and becoming overwhelmed. Again, you might even find yourself procrastinating on this motivation project because it seems too large. By looking at one category at a time and working on that, you'll be breaking it down into a manageable section, just like we talked about in our last chapter on the milestone technique!

Ask Someone Else's Opinion

Once you have your own ideas, it might be a good idea to sit down and have a chat with someone who knows you well, and who you trust. This means you can gain an external perspective, and you might even be given pointers that you had overlooked for yourself.

It's likely that you'll need to speak to more than one person, and it's unlikely that you have just one person who is present in all areas of your life. You might need to speak to a trusted work colleague to find out if they have any other insights into your motivation at work. You could speak to your partner about your personal life. You might like to speak to a close friend about other parts of your life.

The idea of speaking to someone else isn't to change your view of what you've already written, it's about checking to see if you've forgotten anything and gaining a different perspective. We see things through our own eyes but, that doesn't mean that trying to see things through someone else's can bring a few other gems of information our way.

The only thing you need to be careful of is that you choose someone you trust; otherwise you're not likely to take what the say in the spirit is intended, or seriously. By choosing the right person, you can be sure that the whole exercise is worthwhile.

Scribble down any points they make and add them to your original brainstorming paper. This will give you a complete picture.

Acknowledge Your Need to Change And Commit to it

Now it's time to grab a highlighter pen!

Take a look at your brainstorming page and assess each section once more. Which section is most important, i.e. most pressing? Choose the area which has the most work to be done and highlight specifics that stand out. This will focus your mind on areas you need to change.

Part of the battle when changing anything in your life is actually acknowledging and confirming in your mind that you need to make a change in the first place. You have to be firm in what you need to do, and that means total commitment.

So, why do you want to increase your motivation in certain parts of your life? What reason do you have? You need to add meaning; otherwise you're probably going to just slip back into your old ways. Identify a reason why you want to increase your motivation and tell yourself why. If you need to write it down and use it as a mantra or affirmation, go for it, but be sure in your reason and know why you're doing it.

Points to Remember From This Chapter

This chapter has aimed to help you identify your own motivation status and look at the different areas in your life where you might need to do some work.

It's unlikely that you're a completely unmotivated person in every single aspect of your life, but if you are, it's far easier for you to identify what to do as a result! You have to start at the beginning and work your way up in this case. However, it's more likely that you have problem areas in your life and some which are ticking along quite nicely.

By conducting your own personal assessment and acknowledging a need to make changes, you have the information you need to begin.

The main points to take from this chapter are:

- Most people have motivation in some parts of their life, but not in others
- Identifying your problem areas will give you information to start your self-improvement journey

- Sitting down and being open and honest with yourself about motivation problems will give you a clear starting point
- Talking to someone you trust can be useful in helping you see things from another perspective and perhaps pick up items you might have missed
- Acknowledging the problem and being clear in your intention to change will help you overcome hurdles and roadblocks.

Chapter 4:
Start With an Even Foundation

Now you've identified your starting point, do you have the motivation to begin?

That probably seems like an ironic question considering this book overall is about increasing the motivation in your life. However, the fact that you're feeling those bubbles of excitement about making a positive change in your life is something you should take heart from - it shows that motivation can come easily for you, you simply need to feel passionate enough about the task at hand.

In order to succeed and achieve anything in life, you need to have a strong and even foundation to build upon. In this case, you need to look at your lifestyle and the way you think and figure out whether any changes may be necessary. Then, you can work to build upon that foundation with the motivation-busting exercises and tips we're going to continue to give you throughout the book.

Physical And Mental Decluttering For Extra Motivation

In order to focus and concentration clearly and properly, you need to declutter both your physical space and your mental space.

Are you able to concentrate and work accurately and productively when your office desk is cluttered? Probably not. You can't find papers very easily because everything is piled up, your inbox is overflowing and making you feel pressured just looking at it, and you don't have the space to spread out and work properly.

This is a very good example of why it's important to declutter your space if you want to be more productive and if you want to be motivated to actually get more done in the time you have.

When your inbox is overflowing, either physically or electronically, it's very difficult to know where to begin. As a result, you might find yourself procrastinating more, putting things off because you just don't know where to start and it seems too hard to try and work it out. Over time, this makes your inbox even more cluttered, which simply adds to the problem and creates the perfect storm.

The physical clutter also adds to your mental clutter and makes your brain feel all too foggy. That means you can't focus or concentrate, your motivation is non-existent and getting anything done is very difficult indeed.

So, how can you declutter in this way? Focus on one thing at a time. So, focus on physical cluttering and you'll probably find that you'll have less mental decluttering to do as a result.

Physical Decluttering

Start with your work environment. For instance, if you work at a desk, focus on that. If you work somewhere else, focus on that. Any pieces of paper you have on your work surface need to be filed away somewhere specific. A few rules for this include:

- Any pieces of paper which represent a task you can complete in five minutes should be done there and then, and then the paper either discarded of or filed in the appropriate place

- Any pieces of paper which simply need filing away should be filed there and then
- Any papers or books which are reference materials should be kept in an appropriate place, e.g. on a bookshelf, in a box file, or in a filing cabinet
- Any papers which represent larger tasks should be placed on a 'large task' pile
- Any papers which represent medium tasks should be placed on a 'medium task' pile

At the end of your paper decluttering session, you will be left with two piles - your large tasks and medium tasks. For each one, scribble down on a Post-it note which actions need to be taken and place them in your in-tray, labelling them as large or medium. If you want to call them something more identifiable to you, that's fine.

This doesn't mean you're going to leave them there in your in-tray and forget about them, but for now, you're simply decluttering, not scheduling. Once you've finished your physical decluttering, we'll talk about how to schedule your tasks and therefore not procrastinate in a later chapter. Let's stick to the decluttering side for now.

Now you need to look at any other items in your work environment that are causing dust and clutter. Do you have ornaments and other items that are simply collecting dust and don't really serve any purpose? If so, get rid of them. Try and make your space as clear as possible. Sure, you can have the odd family photo but keep it minimal!

You also need to declutter your home environment. This can actually be quite fun because you can identify items you don't use and might be able to sell or donate to a local charity shop. Start with one room and work your way around the house, but be sure to be brutal in what you keep and don't keep - if you don't use it or wear it, and it doesn't fit you or serve a purpose, get rid of it!

This type of physical decluttering has a direct impact on your mental focus and concentration and therefore on your motivation. You're far more able to see the woods for the trees when you're not surrounded by physical clutter. This has a psychological effect of making you feel 'penned in' or suffocated and that in itself is not a very effective picture for feeling motivated to get anything done.

However, as you declutter your physical spaces, you'll probably find that you feel more motivated as you're doing it. The fact that you motivated yourself to declutter is the start of the job - it's a flicker that will turn into a flame if you continue on with your aims.

Mental Decluttering

Physical decluttering will allow you to feel clear in your headspace, but there are other elements to mental decluttering too.

Grab a piece of paper and write down any tasks you need to do which you've been meaning to get around to. Write down anything which is nagging at your mind or bothering you, and basically clear out your brain.

From that list, can you see any tasks that you can complete now, within five minutes? If so, do them and put a line through them. Are there tasks within there which are large or medium? If so, add them to your inbox piles if it's a work issue and if it's a home issue, start a to-do list for each category. Again, we're going to cover a specific technique called 'scheduling' a little later on, which will help you to organise these tasks and therefore motivate yourself to get things done when they come your way and not leave them to pile up and cause delays, forgotten tasks, and missed deadlines.

As part of your mental decluttering efforts, it's a good idea to keep a pen and paper at the side of your bed. We often wake up with a thought in our heads, and we think to ourselves that we won't forget it. We often do, or we stay awake because the nagging in our brains not to forget it is enough to unsettle our night's sleep. Having a pen and paper there means you can scribble anything down that comes to mind and deal with it the following morning.

By decluttering your physical and mental spaces you'll have a firm and even foundation on which to work. The next step is to look at your lifestyle and work out whether you have certain lifestyle habits that are causing motivation problems.

Lifestyle Changes For Extra Daily Focus

Occasionally, it's not what you do that is causing you to be unproductive or struggling to find motivation, it's actually a little deeper than that. It could very well be as a result of your lifestyle and the foundation on which you're living.

If you're not getting enough sleep every night, it's going to be very difficult for you to find motivation for anything. Instead, you're feeling sluggish and tired, and you just want to sit and do nothing. That's not a very productive picture.

You might also be lacking in certain vitamins and minerals as a result of eating a poor diet. In that case, you're not going to feel very energetic and that will certainly affect your motivation levels.

Looking at your lifestyle can often yield some very useful information in terms of how you can fix problems and boost your motivation and energy levels quite quickly. The four main categories to look at are:

- Diet
- Sleep
- Exercise
- Getting rid of unhealthy habits

Let's look at each one in turn and figure out whether there are any changes you can make to boost your energy and motivation levels without really doing much work.

Diet

If you're eating a high sugar diet then you're going to be constantly experiencing sugar highs and lows. When you first eat the sugary snack that you love so much, sure, you're going to notice a boost in energy, but then you're quickly going to notice a crash. This is because your blood sugar has dropped and you're struggling for energy, focus and concentration as a result. Your motivation is basically zero at this point.

The same can be said for eating heavy, fat-laden meals. This simply makes you feel sluggish, and you're not getting much in the way of useful vitamins or minerals as a result.

There are certain foods which you should try and focus on increasing in your diet, including:

- Fatty/oily fish, such as salmon, sardines or trout, which are high in omega 3 fatty acids and can help boost overall brain power
- Coffee, but only in moderation
- Berries, especially blueberries
- Turmeric
- Broccoli
- Pumpkin seeds
- Dark chocolate, again only in moderation
- Nuts, especially walnuts
- Oranges
- Eggs, especially the yolk
- Water
- Green tea

By focusing on healthier options and kicking out high sugar and high-fat options, you'll not only feel healthier, but you'll notice that you're more able to focus and concentrate as a result. This will have a direct impact on your mood and also your motivation levels.

Make sure you drink plenty of water throughout the day and avoid reaching for sugary drinks, even if they say they're 'diet' versions. The 'diet' versions often contain sweeteners that do nothing for health or concentration.

Sleep

Perhaps the easiest way to boost motivation and energy is to make sure you're well-rested! As a rule of thumb, you should be aiming for 7 to 8 hours of sleep every night, uninterrupted and without fail. This might not be the case for you right now and even if you manage it, you might not be able to do it every night. The point is that you're trying.

The biggest issue is that most people work hard throughout the week and then assume that they can sleep in at the weekends. You can see the thinking behind it, but it's actually not at all healthy for your body clock. You need to have a set bedtime and wake up at the same time every morning, regardless of whether you're working or not. This will help you have a set routine and you'll feel more alert and motivated as a result.

If you struggle with sleep, as many people in this day and age do, it could be down to a very simple issue that can be rectified. For instance:

- Avoid watching or listening to anything too stimulating in the couple of hours before you sleep - such as loud music, games, action movies, looking at social media on your phone, etc
- Avoid eating heavy foods too close to bedtime; you should try not to eat in the three hours or so before you sleep if at all possible
- Avoid caffeine-containing drinks before bed. Stick to warm milk or chamomile tea
- Try a warm bath before bed, or the warm drink we just mentioned
- Make sure that your bedroom isn't too hot or too cold; you might like to open the window to get some fresh air
- Are your pillows comfortable? Pillows need to be replaced every year to two years maximum, otherwise, they lose their supportiveness
- Do you have enough blankets? Some people find weighted blankets useful for helping them to sleep, so this is something you might like to try for yourself

These are all ways you can try and get a better night's sleep, but if you do find that you're struggling or that insomnia is a problem for you, have a chat with your doctor and see if there are other treatment options you might find useful.

Exercise

Moving more and getting your blood pumping has some major benefits for your overall health and wellbeing, but it can also help to motivate you to achieve more simply by boosting the blood flow to your brain.

When you exercise, your heart pumps a little faster, and that means that key nutrients and oxygen are making their way around your body more effectively, including up to your brain. This can increase mental performance, memory and motivation at the same time.

You don't have to join the gym and attend every day to find these benefits, you can simply walk to work, park the car a few stops before work and walk the rest of the way, take the steps instead of the lift, and perhaps go for a walk during your lunch break.

If you find that you're enjoying your exercise and feeling the uplifting benefits, you might like to take it a step further, perhaps by going swimming, walking longer, jogging, going to an exercise class, joining a team sport, or maybe joining the gym.

Getting Rid of Unhealthy Habits

Drinking too much, smoking, not exercising, overeating to deal with emotional problems, these are all unhealthy habits that can affect mood, confidence, energy and motivation. These are likely to make you feel pretty sluggish, and that does nothing for your motivation levels.

Instead, focus on identifying these habits and then replacing them with healthier options. Look to cut down and then stop smoking; not only will your health thank you but your bank balance too! Limit the amount you drink and enjoy a glass of wine in moderation instead. Move more and enjoy how it feels, and talk about problems rather than using food as a crutch.

These are lifestyle changes which can take the to achieve and sometimes can be hard to do, but they're all very worthwhile and will allow you to be happier, healthier, more confident, and more motivated as a result.

Of course, it's important to look at your lifestyle and be as healthy as possible, but all work and no play is very dull! This is the same for having a perfect diet 100% of the time and denying yourself the odd chocolate bar as a treat!

Life is about moderation, so if you want a slice of pizza or a bar of chocolate occasionally, that's fine, go for it. All you need to do is make sure that you remember moderation and that you don't repeat the reward the following day and the one after that.

It's very true that a little of what you fancy every so often does you good, and that certainly works for your motivation too. However, that doesn't mean you can use that adage to move towards the unhealthy side of the spectrum every single day!

Points to Remember From This Chapter

This chapter has focused on lifestyle changes you can make to try and increase your motivation levels. In some cases, it can simply be that you're stuck in an unhealthy habit or cycle, and that is drastically sucking the life out of your motivation and your health in general. By being aware of what changes to make, you may find that your motivation starts to increase quite quickly.

The main points to take from this chapter are:

- Your lifestyle can affect many different areas of your life, including how motivated you feel in general
- Focusing on your diet, how much sleep you're getting, how much exercise you do regularly, and rectifying the unhealthy habits you might have developed will help you to feel healthier but will also allow you to increase your motivation too
- Having a healthy lifestyle doesn't mean you can't have the odd treat every now and again, which in itself will help you to stay on track and motivated in your daily life.

Chapter 5:
The Importance of Effective Time Management

Learning how to increase the amount of motivation in your life covers many different elements, as we've already touched upon. We know that your lifestyle can affect how motivated you are, simply by giving you more energy and confidence, but reducing stress can also tie into this.

Stress is a huge motivation killer. If you're stressed, you're just going to feel like there's no point in doing anything and as a result, you'll literally end up doing zero. Then, just as we mentioned in our chapter on procrastination, everything builds up into a picture that is not only stressful and overwhelming but can also cause you to move towards burn out.

When you have too many things to do, it's easier to do nothing. That might sound odd, but putting things off is usually the easier option. It's far more difficult to simply drive on and get started because that requires the big M this book is about - motivation. When you're procrastinating and stressed, motivation falls by the wayside.

There is one thing which can help you overcome this and get a foot onto the mountain you need to climb - Time management.

Time management is a whole subject in itself, but it covers many different techniques that can help you manage your time better, do more in the time you do have, control your workload so you feel more confident and reduce stress in the process. All of this creates more motivation, because the more you do, the more you want to do. It's like a snowball effect.

There are many different ways you can manage your time, and not every single technique will work for you. It's about finding your ideal time management technique and using it whenever you need to. You might also try a few different ones and use them according to the task you have at hand and how you feel on any given day.

In this chapter, we're going to cover five specific time management techniques you can try, but it's important to realise that this isn't an exhaustive list. There are countless more, and you might even create your own. You can take various elements from different techniques and merge them together to create your own bespoke way of managing your time.

We're also going to talk about how all of this ties into the very subject of this book.

Let's start there.

How Does Time Management Increase Motivation?

You might wonder how some of these subjects actually tie in to increasing your motivation, but motivation is a broad and complex subject. Remember, you can't see it and that means there are various different things which create it, keep it going, increase it, decrease it, etc.

Time management methods, when used correctly, help you to do more in the time you have. That puts you in control. So, when you have several tasks to do, you can manage them in a way which means they fit into the hours you have, without having to stress yourself out and work tirelessly, without a break.

That's the other thing people don't tend to realise. If you want to be motivated, you need to give yourself regular breaks!

Taking breaks is not counterproductive, it's actually the opposite. When you have regular breaks, you're giving your brain the time it needs to refocus and recover. You're clearing your mind, and then when you go back to doing whatever you were doing before the break, you can concentrate more clearly. This means you're going to make fewer mistakes, you're going to come up with more creative ideas that can be used within the task, and as a result, it will be completed to a higher standard.

How often should you take breaks? That's a grey area.

If we're talking about work, then employers aren't actually duty-bound to make you take your breaks and they don't have to give you set ones at specific timescales, but they do need to give you a lunch break and they do need to allow you to take breaks when you feel you need them. That basically means the onus is on you to make sure you take them up on this, without going over the top.

You don't need a 20-minute break every hour; that's not going to be very productive, but taking a screen break every hour is a good idea. That means doing a task which isn't related to your computer screen. It could be filing, making some phone calls, or something else which doesn't mean you're sitting in front of a monitor or a laptop screen.

The best rule of thumb here is that if you feel like you're starting to find it hard to concentrate and your motivation to keep going it waning, it's probably time for a break. Grab a drink of water, rehydrate, give it ten minutes and then get back to it. You'll probably find that your focus is better for it.

Of course, when you can manage your time better, taking regular breaks and listening to your body and what it needs, you are less stressed as a result. You'll feel more in control of your workload, whether professionally or personally, and that means you won't fall foul of the procrastination issue we were talking about earlier.

The ironic thing is, when you feel in control of your work, when you plan everything out and you're making steady progress, it actually motivates you to continue and do more. You want to hit those milestones and tick those tasks off your list, it almost becomes like a competition in some ways! Your motivation increases with every item you tick off your list and the more progress you make. Before you know it, you're hitting milestones left, right, and centre, and it feels good!

Time management makes all of this happen because it puts the control back in your hands. You won't feel like someone is stealing hours of the day away from you, and you won't spend your days panicking because you've got too much work and not enough time.

This doesn't mean that you're never going to have days when things go a little awry; perhaps an urgent task comes your way and you have to move a few things onto another day, but you'll have the confidence to deal with that as a result of your increased motivation.

Confidence feeds motivation, motivation feeds productivity. Working on one thing basically means you're working on the whole cycle.

5 Time Management Techniques to Try

A little later in the book, we're going to talk about techniques you can try to boost your motivation, and we're going to go into detail on how to use them in your daily life. Some of those techniques actually overlap with time management techniques to a great degree, so it's important to recognise the similarities at this point and understand why. This isn't a case of repeating ourselves, it's simply that there is such a close relationship between time management and motivation, that it's impossible to deny it or separate them.

However, there are some specific time management techniques that can be used alone and will not only increase your motivation slowly but will also allow you to actually get more done in the time you have.

Let's look at a few in turn.

To-Do Lists And Effective Prioritisation

Everyone knows about the traditional to-do list. This is basically a piece of paper and you write down all the jobs you need to do, ticking them off as you do them. It's a real thrill when you actually tick something off and that in itself motivates you to keep going and tick off more. When you manage to complete your list, you want to do it again the next day and keep the pattern unbroken.

These days, thanks to smartphones, we can now use apps to make to-do lists, so you don't have to rely upon a scrappy piece of paper. These apps are usually all singing, all dancing, and have many different features, such as alarms and time tracking, to keep you firmly on the road to completing your list. It's up to you whether you use an app or you stick with the old fashioned paper version; it's really whatever works for you and personal preference, however, sometimes there is a greater amount of satisfaction in ticking something off manually, i.e. with a pen, than pressing a button on a screen.

It's no good simply writing a list and just ticking items off, you need to take it a step further if you want to increase productivity and motivation along the way. This is where prioritisation comes in.

Prioritising basically means that you choose tasks that are more urgent or more important and you do those first. It's quite easy to prioritise, but it does mean that you need to set aside five minutes at the start of the day in order to do it. Many of the apps we just mentioned will also have this function.

So, look at your list of tasks and number them in order of importance or urgency, with number one being the most urgent or important. You will do that task first and then work down from 1 to whatever.

It's important to point out however that sometimes a prioritised to-do list ends up being thrown out of the window. A little earlier we mentioned the fact that your time management technique of choice can sometimes be challenged simply because a more urgent task has come to you out of the blue. At work, this could be an urgent report, and at home, this could be because the washing machine has suddenly broken and you need to get it fixed ASAP.

When this happens, you need to take a breath, regroup and then look at your list again. Re-organise your list, allowing you to complete the most important task first and moving the others down. It could be that some tasks you simply don't have the time to complete that day and in that case, you can move them on to tomorrow and make them a greater priority a day later. This isn't procrastination, although it does sound like it; the difference is that you have no choice in this situation - when you procrastinate, you always have a choice.

In a working situation, it could also be that you can delegate certain tasks that you can't get around to, or ask for help from your colleagues. At home, you might be able to ask your partner, a family member, friend, or one of your teenage children if they can give you a hand. The key is to manage the situation in a calm manner, finding ways around the problem, without starting to procrastinate, panic, or lose your motivation.

Overall, the to-do list method might be basic, but it's one which is pretty

The Pomodoro Technique

A little earlier we talked about the importance of taking breaks, and the great thing about the Pomodoro Technique is that it incorporates hard work with regular breaks. It basically forces you to have breaks, therefore refreshing your mind and helping you to stay focused.

The technique was developed in the 1980s by Francesco Cirillo. Nobody is quite sure how it got its name, but it's certainly a very effective and very popular time management technique that is used the world over.

Within this technique, you work solidly on a task for 25 minutes, focusing completely. It's a good idea to set a timer to measure how long you're working for. Then after the 25 minutes, you then down tools and have a 5-minute long break. After those 5 minutes, you repeat the 25 minutes of work, then having another 5 minutes break time. The working time is called a Pomodoro, hence the name to some degree.

Once you've had four Pomodoros, you have a longer break, usually between 15 to 20 minutes, before starting the cycle again.

This particular technique helps you quickly establish a rhythm, and because breaks are factored into your time, you don't have to think about them or try and figure out when to take them. The method is also based upon research that states concentrating for 25 minutes is an optimum amount of time, before having a break to allow you to refresh and refocus your mind. The longer break after four Pomodoro sessions gives you the longer regrouping time you need after a while.

It's important that during your break times on the Pomodoro you literally break off from work and you don't just switch tasks. As it's only 5 minutes, it's literally enough time to go to the water fountain and get a drink, make a coffee, or just go to the toilet. That's all you need to regroup and then it's back to work for another 25 minutes of concentration.

The Pomodoro Technique can be very motivating in itself. Because it has a structure to follow, it's easier to do and you're working towards a regular goal, e.g. your break. This motivates you to complete the 25 minutes of work, allowing you to challenge yourself within that time.

This is a very popular method and it's a good idea to try this one out, for sure. You might find that it's all you need to really get on with your working day, or whatever you need to do at home, however, many people use the Pomodoro Technique alongside to-do lists too, simply to keep everything recorded and in one place.

Sometimes when you're juggling things in your mind, it clouds your ability to focus. This is something we talked about in our decluttering chapter, so make sure that you write anything down that pops into your mind and deal with it during a useful time, e.g. a quieter moment. That way, you're not going to be cluttered mentally whilst trying to focus.

Time Challenges

Some people find simply challenging themselves to get a specific task done in a certain amount of time can be very motivating. The reason is that nobody wants to lose! Everyone wants to win and when a challenge is set, the game is on.

However, with time challenges its vital that you don't set unrealistic timescales. If you do this, not only are you setting yourself up for likely failure but you might also be rushing the task to try and finish it, therefore not focusing all your attention on it and making possible mistakes.

However, if you work out a realistic time to finish a specific task and then perhaps shave five minutes off the time, you can challenge yourself to try and meet that target. This is a good option to use when you simply don't like a task that you need to do. Perhaps you have a pile of filing that you have to complete and you really don't like filing. In that case, using the time challenge technique means that you're challenging yourself to get the task done in a realistic time, you're focusing on the challenge at hand, and you're not really focusing on the fact that you don't like filing.

In this case, it's the challenge that people find motivating, but it's best not to try this with a task that you've never done before. You need to know how much time that specific task normally takes you, so you're not setting yourself up for failure. Then, knock a small amount of time off it and see if you can meet the aim.

Give it go, if nothing else it's actually quite good fun!

RPM - Rapid Planning Method

This particular time management method was developed by self-help guru Tony Robbins and it's a way of refocusing your brain to look at tasks in a different way. In this method, you're not focusing on the fact you have to do something and how you're going to do it, you're focusing on the outcome you want. That in itself is motivating because you can already see the outcome, and as a result, you can almost feel the sense of achievement that goes with it.

When you know how good something feels, it's far easier to put the work in to repeat that feeling, and that's what the RPM method is all about.

RPM stands for Results, Purpose, Massive Action and by following the steps you're focusing on the final outcome.

So, when you have a task you need to complete, first ask yourself what result you want, i.e. what outcome do you want. Make sure you make this clear in your mind and say it to yourself. For instance, I want to clear this pile of filing. Then, ask yourself why you want it, giving yourself a purpose and adding meaning to the task. So, the filing could be because you will have a clearer desk and you will be able to declutter a little, whilst acknowledging that will feel good.

The next step is to make an action plan to actually get the job done, and this is the 'massive action' part of the acronym. So, you're going to start at A and you're going to file sections every couple of hours, or you're going to focus on getting from A to K today and you're going to work through your filing from L to Z tomorrow. That is your action plan and it's going to take effort to do it, but your meaning gives you the motivation to work towards your aim.

Next? Do it! Execute your plan, remembering the purpose of your task whenever you start to feel like you're going to procrastinate or you think you could be doing something generally more exciting. Once it's done, the most important thing is to celebrate your success, by giving yourself a pat on the back and perhaps a small reward for your efforts.

The crux of the RPM Method is that it trains your brain to approach tasks in a different way. It makes your brain recognise the sense of achievement and therefore taps into motivation by linking the meaning to the task.

This particular method is a good one for tasks that you really find yourself unmotivated to start. We used the example of filing because not many people relish spending an hour or more doing physical and manual filing, and whilst there's less of this these days, thanks to electronic storage methods, it's still a job that needs to be done in some cases. For that reason, RPM is a good way to find motivation when there is a desired outcome, but not much in the way of motivation to get there before you begin.

The Pareto Principle (also known as the 80/20 Rule)

Our final example of useful time management techniques is the Pareto Method. You might hear this sometimes referred to as the 80/20 Rule also, but it's one and the same.

The basic idea behind the Pareto Principle is that you get 80% of the results from just 20% of the effort. For instance, you would plant a series of bulbs in your garden in the springtime and 80% of the flowers you receive from that yield come from just 20% of the bulbs you planted.

It means you can put in less effort and get more out of it, if you know how to make this method work for you. Put simply, 80% of your overall results come from just 20% of your time and general effort.

The Pareto Principle is about identifying your strengths and weaknesses and working out how to work more effectively. The fact that you're putting in less effort and getting good results is quite motivating in itself, so how do you go about it?

This particular method isn't quite as easy to implement as the others we've talked about so far and does require a little deep thinking beforehand. However, once you've mastered it, you'll tap into some very useful information that you can use in every single task you turn your attention to from this point onwards.

To use the Pareto Principle you need to sit down and be honest about the areas you need to work on, e.g. your weaknesses and then you need to work out where your strengths are. By doing that, you then work to kick out your weaknesses or not focus on them at all, and you use your strengths so you can get more out of them.

As you can see, it takes a little getting used to, but the results are quite far-reaching and once you start using it effectively, the motivation to use it more often will come easily, because you'll see how much more you can do, from quite a lot less in the way of effort

It's Okay to Say "No" Sometimes

It seems that in the current day and age, we don't find it very easy to say "no". We are a society of people pleasers and as a result, we feel that if we refuse to do something, albeit politely, we're going to be vilified or thought badly of.

This isn't the case.

If you cannot do something, if you really don't have the time, then it's perfectly okay to say "no".

A good time management method in itself is learning how to say "no" and being okay with it. This might take a few tries, especially if you're someone who is always agreeing to do things for other people and then finding yourself with far less time of your own. This might seem like you're being a nice and helpful person, but in reality, you're tying yourself up in knots and making life harder for yourself.

Of course, that doesn't mean you can go around refusing to help others all the time, it simply means using your judgement and being honest about the amount of time you have and your ability to complete tasks to the best of your ability. This works for home and work situations - sometimes we say "yes" to everything when family members ask us to do something, but we just don't have the time and we're scared to admit it.

You're not superhuman!

Another thing to mention is multi-tasking. As a result of agreeing to do everything for everyone, you might find yourself trying to juggle different tasks.

Multi-tasking is a huge no-no if you want to get more done in the time you have, avoid stress, and basically find the motivation to focus on the things you need to focus on. You cannot focus on more than one thing at a time properly and without mistakes and it's a total waste of time to try and do two things at once because how can you focus on both things equally, without mistakes?

Instead, choose one task, complete it, and then move on to the next. Not only will you tick something off your to-do list and feel good about it, but that action in itself will motivate you to move on to the next time, feeling good about that.

Motivation is a snowball effect that increases with every action. Encourage it and it will grow. Avoiding multitasking is one way to encourage motivation, for sure.

Why Goal Setting is Vital For Increased Motivation

Do you have any goals? We're not talking about your main life aims or goals, we're talking about daily goals that help you get more done and therefore motivate you to move towards those larger life goals.

Everything is linked, everything in life is connected, and one action towards one thing will either move you further towards it or further away from it. This is why goals are so important.

A great way to motivate yourself in the morning to get on and do whatever you need to do is to set SMART daily goals.

SMART goals are:

- Specific
- Measurable
- Actionable
- Relevant
- Timely

Put simply, you're making goals which are specific, i.e. you've given them a clear meaning and you know what you need to do, you can find ways to measure how effective you are and how much progress you've made, they're relevant to your final aim and you have a timescale to hit.

By doing this, you're more likely to be successful.

Your daily goals can be anything. It can be that you want to cook something new for dinner, pay your rent, clear up your desk, anything. If it's important to you or a task you specifically need to complete, make it a goal at the beginning of the day and work towards completing it. Goals give you something to aim for, and that sparks motivation into life.

Of course, the more you want something, the easier it is to be motivated to achieve it. A little later we're going to talk about visualisation techniques to help you really drum up a desire for an outcome, but you can also tap into the RPM method we just mentioned, giving your aim a purpose and working towards it.

Motivation is far easier to come by than you think, but you have to want the outcome more than actually wanting to do the task itself.

Points to Remember From This Chapter

This chapter has focused completely on time management. When you're in control of the work you need to do, either professionally or personally, you feel less stressed and more motivated to get things done. When you're stressed, it's virtually impossible to focus and therefore motivation goes out of the window, as procrastination creeps in.

By learning how to manage your time better, you'll feel lighter in yourself and that is a great starting point for budding motivation.

The main points to take from this chapter are:

- Time management and motivation work hand in hand
- Learning to take control of your time means you're able to get more done

- There are many time management techniques you can try. Some might work for you, others might not, but once you find a fit that suits you, you can utilise it with great effect
- Learning to say "no" sometimes is the best way to focus and motivate yourself to complete your to-do list
- Multi-tasking will not allow you to be productive and will kill your motivation and productivity levels
- Setting goals can help you to become more motivated because when you attach a meaning to something, it becomes more desirable.

Chapter 6:
15 Strategies to Naturally Boost Your Motivation

Now it's time to get super-practical!

By getting to this point in the book, you've indicated a will and desire to boost your motivation levels and live a happier and more productive life. That's a great choice. You'll certainly feel more in control of your own workload, whether in your personal or professional life, and as a result, you'll notice an increase in your confidence, health, wellbeing, and happiness.

There may be times in your life when motivation seems hard to come by. This might be a short-lived thing, e.g. you just can't get going in the morning one particular day, or it might be a pattern which needs to be broken, e.g. you're having a hard time in one aspect of your life and it's starting to cause you to feel down and affecting your motivation as a result.

The length of time you're experiencing the motivation problem for doesn't really matter, what matters is the effort you put forth to rectify it.

In this chapter, we're going to pull together a list of 15 different strategies you can try to boost your motivation levels naturally. Some of them we've touched upon already, but most are fresh and new introductions.

The general thinking behind all of these processes links back to the theory we've talked about already. The fact remains that if you want something badly enough, you'll be motivated to get the work done and obtain the results and the final outcome. However, to get to that point you need to create a desire and a need to reach the end result.

As with the time management methods we talked about, it might be that not all of these strategies work for you. You might find that a few do and a few don't. You might find that they all do, or you might just find one really high-quality motivation method that ticks every box you need ticking.

There will however something in this list for everyone, but it's a good idea to give them all try and trial them out before making your final choice, or choices. Don't discriminate against any of these choices until you've given them a good try for yourself. If you find it's just not a great fit for you, that's fine; just move on to the next one.

Remember, we're all individuals and that means that one size never fits all. By exploring different options you can find the fit for you which doesn't need any alternations. However, you should also be open to making a few tweaks to specific strategies to help them fit your needs.

It sounds complicated, but it's really not. Once you learn the different strategies we're talking about, you'll see why.

The strategies we're going to explore in a lot more detail in this quite bumper chapter are:

- Visualise The End Goal
- Have a Long Term Plan
- Assess What is Motivating You
- Use Delayed Gratification Methods
- Figure Out Your Most Productive Time of Day
- Use Time Challenges
- Develop a Positive Mindset

- Set Daily and Weekly Goals
- Celebrate Your Successes
- Use Scheduling
- Eat The Frog (not literally!)
- Avoid Overthinking
- Identify Your Personal Mental Blocks And Overcome Them
- Have a Quick Workout
- Bribe Yourself With a Contract

Let's start our exploration now.

Visualise The End Goal

If you've never tried visualisation before, you might need a little time to adjust and get used to the idea and the way it works. Visualisation requires belief, time, effort, and a little perseverance and by giving all of that, you will be rewarded.

Basically, when you're visualising the end goal, you're jumping ahead to the future to explore how something feels, what it looks like, what it smells like, how it feels physically, how it feels emotionally, etc. By doing this, you're putting yourself in the position of already achieving something. When you know how something feels, and presumably it feels good, you want to get there more than anything else.

This, as we mentioned before, is about creating a desire to achieve something and there can be no greater desire than wanting to repeat a feeling that made you feel good.

Visualisation isn't easy and it's something you might need to practice a few times. Many people find it hard to concentrate at first because so many thoughts pop into their heads whilst they're trying to concentrate. It's no surprise really, we live such ultra-connected lives that we're rarely still or calm. Learning to quieten your mind certainly takes time and perseverance, but the results will be quite far-reaching. Once you can learn how to turn off the outside noise, you can become calmer, tap into your subconscious and basically live a healthier life.

So, how do you do it?

Find somewhere quiet, where you're not going to be disturbed, and turn off your phone. There is no greater distraction than the phone ringing or a ping from a notification. Make yourself comfortable. You can either sit or lay down, it's up to you. Get rid of anything which might distract you or take your mind away from what you're trying to focus on.

- Close your eyes and turn your attention to your breath
- Breathe in through your nose for a count of five, in a slow and steady manner
- Be mindful of how your body feels when you breathe in on the inhalation
- Pause for a count of five (three if it's difficult to hold it for five at first)

- Exhale through your mouth for a count of five, in the same slow and steady manner as before
- Be mindful of how your body feels on the exhale and picture tension being pushed away from your body as you exhale
- Repeat this a few times until you feel calm and collected
- When you're ready, bring the task or thing you're trying to picture into your mind
- Let the details settle and try and picture it in as much detail as possible. For instance, if you're picturing what it looks like to move house, try and imagine your house once everything is moved in, where all your furniture is, the pictures on your walls, etc
- Once you've got the picture in your mind, turn your attention to your senses instead. Imagine how it feels, is it warm? Cold? Can you smell anything? Can you hear anything? Try and imagine as much detail as possible and lose yourself in the vision
- If thoughts try and enter into your mind and distract you from your vision, simply let them be, don't pay them any attention and let them float back out of your mind as easily as they float back in

- Once you've got the vision settled in your mind, think about how it feels to have accomplished that task emotionally. Do you feel proud? Tired yet happy? Looking forward to the future? Try and really feel the emotions in the moment as strongly as you can. This will become easier the more you try this exercise
- Be still and live in that moment for a short while, really feeling how great the outcome is
- When you're ready, tell yourself that you're going to leave the visual and turn your attention back to your breath
- After few seconds, open your eyes and sit quietly for a couple of minutes

After you've come back into the room and regained awareness of your surroundings, try and recall the feelings you experienced in that visual. That's what you really need to focus on, because the feelings will be a true motivator to get started and to keep going when things get tough.

You can use this visualisation exercise for anything, but it's best to try it for bigger tasks if possible. By doing this, you're giving yourself something to hang onto, a memory that, although it hasn't actually happened, will push you to keep going and achieve it in real life.

Whenever your motivation starts to waver, which it might at some point, either go back and do the visualisation exercise again, trying to relieve the feelings, or just try and bring a summary to your mind. A quick recap might be all you need to kickstart your motivation and keep going with whatever it is you're trying to achieve.

As we've hinted already, visualisation takes time. It's a little like a simple meditation exercise in many ways, and meditation in itself takes time to master. You might need to practice a few times and you might struggle with trying to keep intrusive thought out of your mind, stopping them from interfering with your visualisation. It will get easier, but you do need to commit to the process and keep trying until you find yourself firmly in that moment and experiencing what it will be like to achieve your end goal before the hard work has begun.

Have a Long Term Plan

It's hard to be motivated to achieve something if you have no clue how you're actually going to get there, or how you're going to do it. It's almost like trying to reach a destination without a map or a GPS - you're basically searching around in the dark, stumbling around and possibly falling over a few times. Once you stumble, you become unmotivated and it's easy to lose your flow.

If you want to achieve something, it's important to have a plan. The larger the task, the more long-term it's going to be. Things take time, and it's no good trying to rush a process that you need to work through slowly.

Again, this is a motivation strategy for large tasks that seem like they're going to take forever. This type of strategy is ideal for things like saving up the deposit for a house, perhaps changing your career, or planning out a travel expedition. The larger the task you want to achieve, the more motivation you need. Of course, that also means you need a larger plan too.

When you make a plan, you'll feel a quick surge of motivation at the start. This is normal and it's something you should take advantage of. When you feel those small motivation surges, ride them like a surfer on a Hawaiian monster wave!

So, how can you make a plan for a large goal or aim?

Firstly, work out what the aim or goal is. Make it very clear in your mind what you want to achieve and be sure that you have it defined. It's hard to be motivated for something that isn't clear. For instance, 'I want to go travelling' is quite a broad statement. Instead, you need to break this down into a more defined and clear idea. Do you want to travel the world? Where do you want to go? Is there a specific way you want to see it? Do you want to visit a specific country?

At this point you don't need to think about how you're going to do something, e.g. the logistics, you simply need to define the idea and make it clear in your mind. If you want to move house, again, that's a broad statement. Instead, define what kind of house you want, e.g. I want to move to a house with more bedrooms, or I want to move to a house in the countryside.

When the goal or aim is clearer, you can start to make a plan.

Your plan should include:

- How long you are going to give yourself to achieve your goal or aim, but do make sure that it's realistic
- How you're going to achieve it, e.g. do you need to save up x amount of money beforehand? If so, how are you going to save the money?
- How are you going to measure your progress? Are you going to have points at which you stop and check how you're doing? If so, how often?
- A plan B. Whilst you might not want to think about 'what if something goes wrong', it's good to have a backup plan just in case something does go awry.

How does this increase your motivation? Because you can see how the whole thing can be from dream to reality. That in itself will give you the motivation to get started, and your plan will keep you on track as you move through each stage. Again, make sure you break your plan down into smaller milestones, to avoid the entire thing feeling so big that it's simply insurmountable.

You might have more than one project going on in your life at any one time, and that's fine. All you need to do however is make sure that you don't have a lot of complicated plans going on, which are going to cloud your mind and make it hard to focus and concentrate.

Of course, it's possible that your plan may change and that's fine. All you need to do at that point, to avoid losing motivation and things flying off course a little, is to sit down and reorganise your plan. Work out what has changed and how you're going to deal with it. Has the plan changed because you no longer want it anymore? Has it changed because for some reason you've become a little unmotivated?

Having regular check-ins with yourself and how you're doing will allow you to find problems before they arise and address anything that might be a minor issue before it turns into something which will knock your plan off course completely.

You also don't have to work on your plan tirelessly every day, but you do need to make sure that you're making slow and steady progress. Rushing things leads to pressure, but being too slow also means that you run the risk of losing interest and forgetting about it completely. Your plan and regular checks in will help you stay on track and keep your motivation high.

Assess What is Motivating You

A little earlier in the book we talked about two specific types of motivation - intrinsic and extrinsic.

You can't really say that one is worse than the other, because we're all motivated by both types in equal measure to some degree. Sure, we do things because we want to, i.e. they bring us pleasure, but we also do things because we want a reward or because we're getting paid, e.g. going to work or trying to hit a target for an end of year bonus. You can't say that one type of motivation is worse than the other because it involves a reward - we all need cash to survive!

What you do need to be careful of however is whether you're motivating yourself to avoid something. If you want to keep your motivation high, it's best to look at what is motivating you and why. By doing that, you can ensure that your positivity is the healthiest type.

So, think of the thing you're trying to do right now. What exactly is your motivation to do it?

Is it because you want to do it, e.g. you find enjoyment from it? Is it because you're going to receive a reward, e.g. money? Is it because it's going to help you achieve a bigger goal?

These are healthy types of motivation, and they're a mix of both intrinsic and extrinsic motivation.

However, if you try and identify what is motivating you and it's something like trying to avoid punishment or trying to stop something from happening, that's not the best way to go about things.

You might wonder why knowing what is motivating you actually boosts your motivation, but it comes down to a healthy mindset. When you're positive and upbeat, you're motivation increases naturally. So, when you're motivated by things which are wholly positive and aimed towards the greater good of you or other people, that's going to help keep that natural motivation high.

However, if you're motivated by trying to avoid a punishment or trying to stop something from happening, that's actually a negative thought, albeit indirectly. Courting negativity doesn't help anyone, and that includes your motivation.

This subject also includes how you motivate yourself. For instance, an example of motivating yourself in a positive way would be "if I finish this task, it will help me move closer to finishing the project completely". A negative type of motivation would be "if I don't finish this task I'm going to feel terrible, and my boss will shout at me".

It's easier to motivate yourself when you're kind to yourself and that means you need to be careful of the type of language you use in your own head. Damaging self-thoughts can lead to a total lack of motivation. So, avoid negative language, avoid forcing yourself to do things and berating yourself it doesn't quite work, or if you fall a little short.

Forgive yourself and appreciate that you're human!

A few examples of words to avoid are:

- Failure/fail
- Any negative words for yourself, such as stupid
- Can't
- Bad

You can see where we're going with this.

Talk to yourself as if you were talking to your favourite person in the world and as a result, you'll notice that you motivate yourself almost without even trying. Negative words do not help, and they force you towards rebellion.

It's far easier to do something when you actually have an interest in it or want to do it. Of course, sometimes we have to do things we don't want to do, but that doesn't mean you can't find some element within it that you find enjoyable. Look for it and focus on that. Avoid talking to yourself in a negative way and make sure that you're not motivated by the need to avoid something or stop something from happening.

If you can tick those boxes, you'll find that you're motivating yourself via a positive means, using positive language to boost your self-confidence, which will naturally help you to move towards your goal, whatever it may be.

Use Delayed Gratification Methods

Now some people find delayed gratification a very unusual method, but when used correctly, it can be a very effective motivator!

What you need to be careful of is that you're not promising yourself rewards for every single thing you do. Delayed gratification should, therefore, be used in moderation only, and for tasks that you really don't want to do, but you need a little nudge to get started on, before moving towards completion.

So, what is delayed gratification?

You basically do a deal with yourself. You might say "I'm finding it hard to concentrate on this report, but if I finish it by the end of the day then I will treat myself to a takeaway for dinner later".

Basically, you're forcing yourself to do something you don't really enjoy by promising yourself a reward of something you do like.

Is this extrinsic motivation? Yes in many ways it is, but its a very useful way to get yourself moving when nothing else seems to be working!

If you're someone who is quite prone to procrastination, delayed gratification is a very useful tactic to help you with specific tasks that have you on the cusp of procrastinating. All you need to do is notice and acknowledge that you're about to procrastinate and put something off until a later time, understand that doing so is going to cause you problems later, and in order to get around the 'do I/don't I' scenario in your head, you make a promise to reward yourself upon completion. The key there is 'upon completion'. Do not give yourself any reward before you've finished the task otherwise you're not going to be motivated to complete it!

The rewards you give yourself when using delayed gratification don't have to be large, in fact, it is better if they're not. If you go around promising yourself large rewards every time you do something you were going to procrastinate on, you're doing to be rather poor at the end of it and then larger treats won't hold the same special meaning.

A few ideas for delayed gratification rewards include:

- A takeaway at the end of the day
- A chocolate bar you like
- A glass of wine in the evening

Useful instant gratification rewards are not things like a new outfit, a new bag, a new computer console, a new phone, or anything which is a large purchase. Do not let your motivation hinge on purchasing large items which could a) cause you to be seriously out of pocket and b) basically be a smokescreen for the fact you were going to buy something you probably can't really afford but you needed an excuse to be able to do it and feel better about it!

There is a difference between delayed gratification and instant gratification. The instant version is when you give yourself the reward before you've finished something and we've already mentioned that's not a good route to go down. The fact that you're delaying the reward is almost like the carrot dangling in front of your nose, wiling you to keep going and do something. It's only when you finish the task that you're near enough to reach out and snatch that carrot away.

This means that you not only get the benefit of having completed the task and avoiding putting it off and making the next day more difficult, but you have the joy to look forward to of whatever reward you've chosen for yourself.

A few of the benefits of using the delayed gratification method are:

- This method helps you to avoid impulsive decisions to procrastinate and put things off
- It helps you to complete tasks and be more productive
- It teaches you that hard work is worth it
- By completing tasks and noticing how good it feels, you'll find that procrastination isn't worth it and instantly recognise the positive vs negative feelings associated with each method
- It helps you to avoid feeling guilty when you've basically taken the 'easy way out' and put off a task until another day
- It motivates you and therefore helps you to feel better about yourself

Some people don't agree with delayed gratification because they believe that you shouldn't have to promise yourself a reward or a treat in order to do something you don't want to do. Of course, understanding that hard work isn't always enjoyable is key, but if promising yourself something small helps you get over a hurdle that you would otherwise have struggled with, is there really any harm?

In some ways, delayed gratification isn't ideal for children or young people. We tend to use it as a bribe in some ways. For instance, we would say 'do your homework and you can have some chocolate'. Of course, it gets them to do their homework, but we shouldn't be using treats as a way to force them to do something which they need to learn to do naturally. However, you're an adult and not a child and you understand that background information more clearly than they do.

For that reason, instant gratification in this kind of situation isn't damaging. What you need to be careful of however is that you're not using it for every situation, otherwise you're going to find yourself falling into a task and reward state of mind. Motivation needs to grow naturally, and opting for rewards all the time basically means that you're using them as a crutch. So, the best advice is to use this method sparingly, but use it whenever you feel like you're really on the edge of procrastination, and you know that a quick promise to yourself will help you overcome it, and finished whatever task is becoming such an issue in that moment.

You might find that you already use instant gratification in some ways already, probably quite naturally without even thinking about it. Most of us do, but being more aware of this as a motivation-boosting tactic will help you get the most out of it and complete tasks without them becoming a larger problem at some point in the near future.

Figure Out Your Most Productive Time of Day

We all have times during the day when we're less motivated and less productive than others. This will vary from person to person, as we're all totally individual.

Some people are full of energy first thing in the morning and they find that their motivation is naturally quite high at this time, before starting to decrease a little as the day goes on. Other people are totally sluggish first thing in the morning, but find they are more productive after lunch, or maybe in the early evening.

When are you more motivated and more productive?

It might help you to keep a motivation diary and find out your best time of day. Keep this for a week and then look back over it to find out your results. All you need to do is sit at the end of every day and think back over how you felt throughout that day. Separate your day up into these sections:

- First thing in the morning, e.g. the first two hours of your day after waking up
- Mid-morning, up until lunchtime
- After lunch
- Mid-afternoon
- Early evening

Rate your motivation and your productivity as one, and use a scale of 1 to 5, with 1 being low and 5 being high.

Over the course of a week, you'll be able to see a pattern emerging and this will allow you to identify the times of the day when you're naturally more motivated and therefore more productive than others. You can use the methods we're gradually exploring to help boost your motivation during the naturally lower times of your day, but during those high motivation times, you can try and do tasks that require more focus and attention.

For instance, if you find that you're more productive after lunch and you take a little while to get going in the mornings, you can schedule in lower energy tasks for that time. So, in the morning you would do tasks that don't really need that much concentration. In a working situation, this could be answering emails, doing some filing, a little photocopying, and generally tidying up your to-do list. Then, when you reach the point of the day when you're naturally more energetic, more motivated and more productive, you can complete the tasks that need more focus and concentration.

There are many benefits to this because it ensures that fewer mistakes are made, and you're getting the most out of the specific times of your day when you don't need to force your motivation. Of course, that doesn't mean you should simply allow your motivation to be lower at other times, but perhaps you can use these lower energy times to regroup. If you push yourself all the time, you're going to end up exhausted and overwhelmed.

Knowing your most productive times, therefore, helps you get more out of your day in a natural way. Ironically, by doing this, you'll have more energy because you're not forcing yourself to try and complete high-focus tasks when you're lacking in motivation and perhaps naturally lower in energy and you're conserving it for the times when you know you're mentally sharper by routine.

However, if you find that you need to shift your most productive time, e.g. maybe you have a presentation first thing in the morning, then you can use the other methods we're going to cover, and the ones we've already talked about, to boost your natural motivation and effectively move your naturally most productive time to the part of the day when you need it the most.

In the end, you have control over all of this, and it could be that you need to make some changes to your lifestyle to actually alter the time of day when your natural energy levels peak. For instance, if you don't get enough sleep on a regular basis, you cannot expect for mornings to be a very productive time for you! Your motivation will be low because you're tired and you're likely to make mistakes as a result. However, if you focus on getting more sleep and perhaps eating a high energy breakfast, containing slow energy release foods, you might find that your energy, motivation and productivity levels rise a little compared to where they're at currently, and you can, therefore, get more done at that time.

The same can be said for the afternoons. If you don't take your lunch break, if you sit at your desk when you should be having a break or if you don't get outside and have some fresh air, you're not going to be that motivated to do much during the afternoon because your energy levels will plummet as a result. However, if you make it your aim to have your lunch at a specific time, eat healthy, high energy foods, and you go outside for a walk in the fresh air, you will probably find that your motivation is naturally higher after lunchtime and could even get you through to the end of your working day.

Changing your lifestyle can have a major effect on your motivation, as we talked about in our earlier chapter on this very subject. It's important that you take a clear look at your lifestyle as it is now and compare this to your motivation and productivity diary, e.g. the times of day when your levels are naturally higher.

Identify some changes to make as a result of this diary and then continue to keep it for another week to ten days. Compare the two diaries and see if there have been any changes. The likelihood is that you have more energy at times of the day when you didn't before, thanks to those tweaks in your lifestyle.

Use Time Challenges

We talked about time challenges in our time management technique, but if you want to increase your motivation by tapping into your competitive side, these challenges are a fantastic way to do just that. For that reason, let's place it here on our list of motivation-boosting methods and cover it in a bit more detail, with some examples to show you how to use time challenges in the most effective way possible.

Everyone has a competitive side, but some people are more competitive than others. If you're one of those people, in particular, this method could be a great choice for you. Even if you're not particularly competitive, challenging yourself might trigger your competitive side and force you to achieve more, without actually realising it.

The great thing about giving yourself a challenge is that it really makes you feel fantastic when you achieve your aim. The key is not to fail, but you're not going to set yourself up for failure to begin with, so the chances of that happening are very slim anyway.

Time challenges can be used for any task which you find difficult, which doesn't really interest you, or a task which you want to get finished quickly, so you can focus on something else. These challenges are also useful when used in conjunction with the milestone method we talked about earlier.

When you have a large task to complete, we explained that breaking it down into smaller milestones makes it seem more achievable and therefore you'll find it easier to motivate yourself to get on with it. If you add time challenges into this, you will boost your motivation because you not only have smaller millstones to complete, which is easier to do, but you'll also challenge yourself to complete it in a shorter timespan, which helps you to achieve the overall task quicker. Of course, that means the entire task, e.g. the one which all the milestones are leading up to, is also completed faster too.

The problem with time challenges is that you can easily use them in the wrong way. You need to be sure that the time you've set aside is realistic. Yes, you can shave a little time off and motivate yourself to try and achieve it faster, but you shouldn't try to achieve it in a time which is unrealistic and totally unachievable. The best-case scenario here is that you complete it, but you make mistakes and therefore reduce the quality of your work. The worst-case scenario is that you miss your deadline and you feel terrible about it, therefore reducing your overall motivation as a result.

As we mentioned before, time challenges are best used for tasks that you've done before, so you have some prior knowledge of how long it normally takes to complete them. This will give you the reliable information you need to work out what your time aim is.

For example, if you want to use the time challenge method for inputting a batch of data, you first need to look at how much data you need to input and work out how long this has taken you in the past. If you have 20 sets of data to work on, and in the past 10 sets has taken you one hour, it's going to take you two hours to do the 20 sets. However, you could then say 'okay, I'm going to do these 20 sets in 1 hour and 45 minutes'.

That isn't shaving too much time off, to the point where it's going to damage the quality of your work and possibly cause you to rush and make mistakes, but it is going to give you something to work towards, and something to kickstart your competitive spirit.

Then, when you're working on that task, keep the challenge in your mind. Keep checking the clock and working out how much time you have left and whether you're on target. Push yourself to reach it, and if at all possible, see if you can make it even less time, without making mistakes.

Triggering your competitive spirit is a fantastic way to boost motivation because by nature we want to win! We want to get things done and when we achieve something special, e.g. doing something in a short amount of time, it feels good! Feeling good is addictive, so focus on what that feels like and work towards meeting that time challenge aim.

We do have to mention what happens if you fail to meet your target. Sometimes this might happen because halfway through your task, when you're working hard and you're on track, almost there, another task might come your way which is super-urgent and you have to down tools and change your focus to that task instead.

In this case, you haven't failed and you should not use words like 'failed', as we've already talked about! Accept the situation for what it is and work out how much work you've done on the prior task and how much is left to do. You've already done some of it, so what is left is going to be less pressing than before. In that case, can you delegate the rest of the task to someone else to do? This frees you up to focus on the new task, and the old task is still competed and not weighing heavily on your mind.

If you can't delegate it, promise yourself that you'll finish it off tomorrow, and work out how much time you'll need, making a new time challenge.

The only time when this method is detrimental is when you approach it with unrealistic eyes. Do not try and do a task that regularly takes one hour in just 20 minutes. It's not realistic, it's not going to happen, and it's going to cause you to lack motivation for the rest of the day because you didn't manage it. It's also likely to cause you more work because you'll make mistakes and you'll need to go back over it and rectify those issues.

Keep everything realistic and work towards beating your own standards.

Develop a Positive Mindset

Positivity and motivation as so closely linked that it's vital you try and adopt a generally positive mindset if you want to get more done in the time you have. It's not possible to be motivated if you're extremely negative. The negativity naturally sucks the will to achieve right out of you and as a result you'll find it far easier to become stressed and overwhelmed because motivation has gone AWOL.

Put simply, negativity and stress cannot live side by side with motivation. They're not good neighbours.

However, positivity and motivation adore each other! It's a real-life love affair that you can tap into and reap major rewards as a result.

As humans, we're programmed to be negative first and positive later. It dates back to the prehistoric days when cave people had to run away from scary-toothed animals to stay alive. This is when the 'fight or flight' stress response was established, and it's stuck with us ever since. In that case, thinking on the dark side was vital for survival, because you never knew what danger lurked around the corner.

Thankfully we don't face the same terrifying threats these days, but our evolutionary mechanisms haven't quite caught up. We're still always on the lookout for the next thing to cause us a drama or harm, and that means that negativity is our default setting.

It can be changed however, you simply need to learn how to rewire your brain a little. The side effects of becoming more positive are extremely far-reaching and very beneficial. You'll be healthier, happier, you'll be more productive, you'll have better relationships with those around you, you'll exude a sense of radiance simply by smiling and having that glass half full approach to life, and yes you guessed it, you'll have more motivated naturally too.

This motivation and brighter outlook will help you to find new opportunities in life almost without trying. And the fact that you're a little more daring these days, thanks to that positive outlook, means that you're going to keep moving through those opportunities, bettering yourself and having new experiences. You wouldn't have done any of this if you'd remained a Negative Nancy or Nick.
So, how can you learn to become more positive? Firstly, you need to accept that it's going to take time and you're not going to notice results

overnight. Do not become disheartened if you don't suddenly wake up feeling full of promise after a couple of days! This is a snowball effect that will shock you at how quickly it appears but might feel like it's taking a while.

It's a contradiction in many ways!

Once you know that it's a process that may take a little time, you need to arm yourself with various strategies:

- Use positive affirmations
- Try reframing your negative thoughts into positive ones
- Try mindfulness

These are just three very effective ways to become more positive and therefore naturally increase your motivation. Let's look at each one in turn.

Positive Affirmations

Affirmations are a great way to programme your brain to believe something which you didn't before. The key is in the repetition, but also in really believing the words you're saying to yourself.

If you want to become more positive and increase your motivation, that's what you need to tell yourself and you need to word it in a quick, short and snappy affirmation that you can repeat to yourself a few times every day. A few examples are:

- I am positive, I'm motivated, I will succeed
- I am strong and I am able
- With every day my motivation is increased

Or, you can make up your own. That's the beauty of affirmations, they don't follow any rules and they can be anything you want them to be.

Once you've settled on an affirmation that really resonates with your aim and what you feel, you need to write it down somewhere and keep it close to you. If you can memorise it, that's even better. After that, you need to say the affirmation three times when you wake up in the morning, another three times at some point during the day, and three times before you sleep. The key here is not only the repetition but really feeling the words you're saying. You have to believe them otherwise there's no point; if you don't believe what you're trying to work towards then positivity and motivation won't come your way and you're basically wasting your time speaking words that don't mean much to you.

However, if you choose your words wisely, focus on them, feel them and repeat whenever you feel you need to increase your motivation and your positivity levels, you will over time notice that you feel not only more upbeat and positive but that you're more motivated naturally.

Reframing

Reframing negative thoughts into positive ones is a very useful and popular cognitive behavioural therapy method (CBT). This is another method that takes time and it's quite a tiring exercise because it means you need to be mindful of every negative thought you're having. You also need to acknowledge those thoughts and identify them as being negative and therefore not of any use to you.

The idea here is that you recognise a negative thought and you replace it with a positive one, repeat it and then allow it to take the place of that original bout of negativity.

An example of reframing looks a little like this, but do remember that it can relate to absolutely any negative thought at all.

- It is summer and you're having a heatwave. The weather is extremely hot and sweaty. You automatically think "I hate being this hot"
- You would then need to recognise this thought as negative because you're using words such as 'hate'. Say to yourself 'I am having a negative thought'
- Once you've acknowledged that negative thought you now need to come up with a positive alternative. An example could be 'the sun gives me important vitamin D'. Again, it can be anything and this is just a random example
- Feel the heat and repeat the positive thought a few times. It's best if you can say it aloud but if you can't because of where you are, in your head is fine
- Focus once more on the heat and repeat the new positive thought once more

The next time you feel hot you're more likely to think of the new, positive thought before the negative one. Again, it might not happen overnight and it could be that you have a quick flash of the negative before correcting yourself with the new positive one, but over time it will replace it. That means the negativity you had towards the sun has been reframed towards positivity.

Over time you'll find this method easier to use and it won't be quite so exhausting, as negative thoughts will become easier to identify too.

In terms of your motivation, you can also use this method to help beat procrastination. So instead of thinking 'I really don't like this task', you should change it to 'completing this task means I will move closer to completing my daily aims'.

Absolutely any negative thought can be reframed. You simply need to be creative!

Mindfulness

Some people think that mindfulness makes you become more passive than motivated, but that's not always the case if you use it in the right way. Mindfulness is a fantastic method for becoming more positive, but also for helping you to live in the here and now, and not constantly be jumping back to the past or thinking ahead to the future.

Mindfulness can be used in conjunction with mediation or it can simply be a way of life that you adopt of your own. It simply means that you take the time to smell the roses, becoming mindful of what is around you, rather than just letting things pass you by and not really taking the time to live in the moment or experience what is around you.

If you're someone who is guilty of living in the past or being fearful of the future, to the point where you don't really live in the moment you're in, mindfulness is a good choice and it's easy to begin with too. All you need to do is take the time to head outside into nature and really take in what is around you.

So, go for a walk, or walk to work the next day without taking the car. Take a deep breath and look around you. Be mindful of the trees and how they look to you, the colours on the leaves, the sound of the wind rustling the branches, and the birds tweeting in their nests. Notice the clouds in the sky and the different shapes they're making, and how slowly they move overhead. Notice the grass and the different shades of green, the flowers growing and anything else which is in the picture you're observing.

The key is to lose yourself in the moment and experiencing the smaller things. The things you wouldn't normally even notice. By doing this, you're turning your attention inwards.

The more you do this, the more you develop a greater appreciation for the smaller things in life, the smaller joys that we often pass by in favour for material goods or other huge experiences that take forever to achieve.

Becoming more mindful makes it easier to deal with stressful situations, it can make you happier, healthier, and as a result of all of this, it can make you more motivated to achieve the things you want to achieve.

Yet again, this takes time, and it's going to be something which is a real slow burn. However, stick with it because the results, when they start to come your way, will be quite impressive.

These three methods help you become more positive in general, but that has very firm links with your motivation. The way you feel when you're upbeat and positive means it's far easier to push yourself to do more, work towards your goals, and get to where you want to be, without procrastinating and beating yourself up for not hitting targets that were never possible in the first place.

Set Daily and Weekly Goals

In our time management chapter, we talked about the importance of having a goal and how that creates a greater sense of motivation. Now we need to talk about how using daily and weekly goals can keep you moving towards larger end goals, and how this can create a sense of positivity and motivation for you every single day.

If you look at the app store for your particular phone or tablet, you'll find several different apps that pertain towards goals, aims, and to-do lists. It doesn't matter which one you choose, or whether you opt for the old paper and pen version, but you need to have a record of what you want to achieve, and you need a way of ticking it off to create a sense of achievement.

There are two ways to do this - you can either create a weekly set of goals that you work through every day until the end of the week, or you can set daily goals. Either option works in the same way. You can even work towards using both, allowing you to stay firmly on target.

For the purposes of this example, let's set a series of weekly goals and explain how this method works.

Sit down and think about the things you want to achieve that week. What tasks can you complete that will help you feel uplifted and positive, but which will also move you closer towards a final aim you have or an end goal? It's a good idea to have a combination of feel-good tasks you want to complete and tasks that will take you closer towards a bigger goal.

For instance, you might have the following task examples on your list:

- Pay electric and water bill
- Buy a birthday gift for your niece
- Book your flights for next month's holiday
- Pick up a prospectus from your local college, with new courses for next term

- Brainstorm ideas for next week's work presentation
- Finally finish the ironing

It doesn't matter how many tasks you have on your list, you can have more or you can have less. What matters is that you have a variety of tasks that move you forwards, whilst also decluttering your mind and helping you to make general progress.

From that list, we have a good balance. You need to pay some utility bills and that is an important task that will be playing on your mind. By writing it down and then ticking it off once you've completed it, you're clearing that from your mind and achieving something important. You also need to buy a birthday gift for your niece, and that's sure to be nagging at the back of your mind, as you try not to forget!

You need to finish the ironing, because it's been sat that, cluttering up your physical and mental space for the last few days, and you know that by completing it you'll feel good and have clean clothes to wear.

The other three entries on your list are helping you to move forwards towards larger goals, both professionally and personally. They're milestones in which a larger task has been broken down into.

For instance, you're going on holiday next month and you're yet to book your flights because you're trying to get the best deal. You've decided that you've waited long enough and this week you're going to book them. The following week you'll start to look for a hotel, moving forwards to completing your holiday planning.

You're also going to go to the college and pick up a prospectus because the new course list is out and you're thinking of retraining to change your career in the next couple of years. Picking up a prospectus means that you're taking small steps towards looking for a course, enrolling, starting it and becoming qualified in your new career.

Finally, you're going to brainstorm ideas for next week's presentation, because you want to be prepared and a slower approach to this large task serves you better.

As you tick each item off, you're helping your daily life run a little smoother, you're making progress at work for next week, and you're starting to move towards your larger life goals at the same time.

This will continue the motivation onwards so that you can keep making slow and steady progress. You'll experience a rush of adrenaline and happiness as you tick each item off too, which will be the catalyst to continue.

So, what happens if you can't tick an item off? Do you feel bad about it? Do you allow yourself to become demotivated? No. You simply make sure that there's a good reason for this and that you've not fallen foul of procrastination and you make it a priority for next week instead. That way, you're not forgetting about it, you're not allowing it to simply be lost in the melee, you're just recognising the sometimes life becomes unexpectedly busy, and that you'll get around to it a few days later than you planned.

That is fine, and as long as you're not simply putting the task off because you don't want to do it, there's no reason to worry!

Setting goals in this way tend to become a little bit of an addiction but in a good way! The more items you tick off your goal list, the better you feel, and the more motivated you are to continue in the same vein and keep ticking things off. You start to feel in control of what you need to achieve, and this pushes you to try and do more.

Celebrate Your Successes

One of the best ways to increase your motivation is to celebrate the things you achieve. All work and no play makes for a very dull life indeed, and if you're constantly doing things and not stopping to pat yourself on the back, it's going to become tiresome, to say the least.

Whenever you achieve something notable, make sure that you celebrate it in some way. This doesn't mean spending a large amount of money or doing something extravagant, it can simply be giving yourself the afternoon off and doing something you enjoy, having a hot bath and watching a film, or perhaps cooking your favourite meal. Celebrating doesn't have to be about excess, it can simply be about self-care. When you focus on yourself and do the things you enjoy, it's going to put you in a far better frame of mind to continue ticking boxes and motivating yourself to move forward.

If you look at the opposite situation, you can clearly see why celebrating your successes become a great motivating tactic to use.

Let's just suppose for a second that you're a self-employed worker and you have many tasks you need to complete before the month is over. Every task is a different set of work for a client, so when you finish one task, you tick that box and then move on to the next, working through these in order of importance or taking note of how close the deadline is.

By doing this, sure, you're making progress towards clearing up your workload and ensuring that you hit all your deadlines, and that's to be commended, but you're simply ticking boxes and working yourself into the ground. By doing this, where is the fun? Where is the motivation coming from? If you continually work, work, work, without any pat on the back or giving yourself a break occasionally, you're going to find that not only do you feel tired, overwhelmed, and run down, but you're also going to notice that your motivation at some point is going to hit a wall. You're going to run out of steam.

So, a better option, in this case, would be to plan out your work, but also incorporate downtime and small pats on the back along the way. For instance, incorporate your work into the week but make sure that you have a day off, make sure that you do something in the evenings that you enjoy, and when you finish one task, give yourself a few hours doing something you love, as a reward for hitting that deadline.

Give yourself a break! Recognise the hard work you're putting in and that in itself will motivate you to continue in the same pattern. If you constantly work, work, work and you don't pause to look at what you're achieving, it doesn't feel fulfilling and it's not at all motivating.

It's important to enjoy what you do. Of course, we go to work for money, but we also need to work in something that we find joy in, something meaningful, and something which allows you to be challenged by the right amount, without pushing yourself into stressful territory which easily begins to affect your health and wellbeing.

Celebrating your successes can be anything you like, but you simply need to make sure that you do it. It can be very easy to carry on working because you tell yourself that if you carry on and do just a little bit more work, you can hit another milestone and you can tick another box. Yes, this is important, but your health and wellbeing is even more important.

You will lose motivation if you don't take the time to recognise what you're doing and say 'well done' to yourself.

We should also take a slight detour here and mention what you should do to motivate your employees in the workplace. If you are a manager reading this book, perhaps looking for ways to motivate yourself, how about giving your employees a dose of second-hand motivation too? This will seriously boost productivity in the workplace, boost morale, and help your employees feel like they're valued and taken seriously.

It's the easiest thing in the world to do and all it takes is a 'well done', or a 'thank you'. Basic manners and basic human decency, that's all it takes!

We don't get thanks for the things we do often enough, but just one word of gratitude can be a huge motivator. It makes us want to hear it more, so we do more in order to try and reach that outcome. In many ways 'thank you' is the perfect motivator!

So, if you're an employer, make sure you add a dose of motivation by thanking your employees for what they do, and if you're self-employed or you're simply trying to find ways to motivate yourself to do more of what you need to do, thank yourself for the focus and hard work you're putting in. Pat yourself on the back, and when you achieve something, no matter whether it's big or small, celebrate it and realise that you've succeeded in doing something that if you'd decided to procrastinate on, you would never have managed.

Be kind to yourself and motivation will follow!

Use Scheduling

The next motivation boosting method we're going to look at is another overlapping time management method, but it's a great way to ensure that you don't miss anything, that you find time for everything you need to do, and you feel in control at the same time. Scheduling also gives you a very clear picture of what you need to do and the work you have already factored in, and this ensures that you're not accidentally demotivating yourself by trying to do too much in an unnatural amount of time.

How does this increase motivation? Because you will easily be able to make headway in whatever you need to do, and that will motivate and push you to try and do more. This method doesn't have simply pertain to a working situation, it can be something you can use in your personal life too.

Scheduling basically means that instead of trying to remember to do tasks, perhaps keeping them writing down on a list or in your head, you actually find a time to do them when you're given that task, or when you identify it. This means that you're not constantly trying to remember a million things, items and tasks don't get put on a list and then accidentally forgotten, and as a result, you're the one who is in complete and utter control.

Let's give you an example of what scheduling looks like from a work point of view, and then from the point of view of your personal life, so you can see how you might be able to use it in your life.

You're at work and you have several tasks written down on your notepad that you need to do over the coming days. Normally, you look at your list every day and identify what you can do that day, crossing items off as you go. Instead of doing that, with scheduling you would avoid writing tasks down and telling yourself that you'll do them later on; instead, you find a time to do them.

Having a scheduling tool is a great method here, and you can download a calendar onto your phone or tablet, or you can opt for a paper-based diary. It's really whatever works for you.

So, look at the tasks you need to do and find a time to do them. Once you've identified and available time slot, write that task in there and block out the time so nothing else takes over that slot. If you need to travel in order to complete this task, make sure you factor that in and estimate a necessary and realistic amount of time that the task is going to take to complete.

Then, when the time actually comes, do it! Make sure you finish whatever is on your calendar or in your diary for that day. It's hugely motivating to see what you need to do and then be able to do it, without stress or panic.

So, in your working situation, you would look at your electronic work calendar and you would block out time for specific tasks. For instance, if you need to travel across town to attend a meeting, you would block out the length of time the meeting takes, plus a realistic amount of time for travelling there and back.

You would look at the rest of the time you have available during the day and add tasks to do during that time, ensuring that you give yourself enough space to be able to have lunch, catch up on admin, etc. It's also a good idea to avoid packing days full of tasks, just in case something urgent comes along and throws your schedule a little out of whack.

By doing this, you're never missing deadlines, and tasks aren't sitting around waiting for a time to be picked up and done. You find a time to do it whenever it comes your way.

In a personal life situation, you can use the exact same method. You might not use an electronic calendar, but as we said before, you can easily download a useful calendar app onto your phone or use a paper diary.

Perhaps your eldest child has a birthday party coming up and you need to drive them across town and then go and pick them up afterwards. You also need to pay the electric bill in town that day and run a few basic errands.

To make sure you don't miss anything, you'd look at that particular date in your diary or on your calendar and you'd block out the right amount of time to take your child to the party and to pick them up. You would also schedule a realistic amount of time to go into town and pay your electric bill and do the other errands. The rest of the day is yours to do whatever you want to do with.

Of course, when using scheduling in your personal life, it's not going to be as prevalent as it would be in your working life. You will schedule on a daily basis at work, simply because you have tasks to do every single day, maybe you have meetings to attend, presentations to prepare and give, etc.

At home, you may simply have a few tasks you need to do on a-specific days, so writing them down in your diary or on your calendar and scheduling a specific amount of time shows you what else you can do on that day, how long it's going to take you and ensures that you don't forget and end up running around in a crazed stress, having just remembered what you need to do.

Scheduling is motivating because it shows you a clear picture and it helps to declutter your mind. You don't have to try and remember anything because it's already there in front of you, and when you complete tasks, simply change the colour of it on your app or place a tick at the side of it in your diary. That simple 'crossing off' action will give you a boost or morale/feel-good factor and will motivate you to try and achieve the same feeling the following day, or the next time you've scheduled something into your diary.

Try it and see how it works for you. It's an ideal way to stop endless lists of things you need to try not to forget, and it helps you feel more in control as a result.

Eat The Frog (Not Literally!)

The name of this particular motivation method might seem worrying, but don't worry, you're not actually eating frogs or anything else for that matter!

Eat the frog basically means that you get the things you don't like, or the tasks you least enjoy, out of the way earlier in the day, and that stops them from becoming a motivation blocker for the rest of your time.

This method is also fantastic for helping you to stop procrastinating. It sounds better than 'bite the bullet' but that's basically what it means - you're getting it over and done with, out of your mind and you're freeing yourself up to do more.

If you think back to the last time you had a task that you really didn't like, or one which just seemed quite boring, how did you feel once it was over? Did you feel quite light and happy that you'd done it? Did it make you feel motivated to get something else done that day because you were positive about what you'd already achieved?

That's what Eat The Frog is designed to do.

The name of this method can from Mark Twain. He said, "if it's your job to eat a frog, it's best to do it first thing in the morning". Of course, nobody really wants to actually eat a frog, it's a task you would try and avoid, procrastinate on even. In this case, Twain means that if you really have to do it, if you have no choice, it's best to do it first thing in the morning and not have it on your mind for the rest of the day, zapping away at your positivity and causing you to feel zero motivation, because you simply can't focus on anything other than the frog-eating you need to do.

Twain also said, "if it's your job to eat two frogs, it's best to eat the biggest one first". The same thought process applies here. If you have two jobs you really don't like, do the biggest one first and get it out of the way. You'll be glad you did and that positive feeling will boost your motivation naturally.

Taking the plunge, biting the bullet, eating the frog, whatever you want to call it, the thinking is basically identical. By doing this task first, the rest of your day is going to be easier, lighter, and more enjoyable, and you'll feel accomplished that you did it, building momentum and therefore motivation for the rest of the day ahead.

So, how can you tell what your personal frog is?

It will be pretty easy to spot. It's probably a task you've procrastinated on a few times already, and it's the task that when you think about it, you get a 'urgh' feeling or a sinking feeling. It's the task you don't like doing, put simply. These types of tasks leave you with zero motivation because it's not an enjoyable experience, however, when they're done, it helps you feel far better.

These are the tasks that are normally left until the end of the day, simply because you would rather do anything else first, but that leaves you with little time to get them done. As a result, you might start and then down tools, or you might put it off until the next day, therefore giving in to the perils of procrastination.

To help you identify that troublesome frog in the room, look at your to-do list for the day and try and mentally break it down into categories. Those categories should be:

- The tasks that you really don't enjoy or like to do but they're important and need to be done
- The tasks that you quite enjoy and also need to do because they're important
- The tasks you quite enjoy but the ones that aren't actually all that important
- The tasks that you don't really enjoy, but you don't really need to do them either

Which do you think is the frog from that list?

You guessed it - the frog is the task that you don't really enjoy and don't like to do, but the one which needs to be done.

It's always the way, right?

However, by approaching the frog with a 'do it and get it out of the way' mindset, you can overcome the issue and feel better throughout the rest of the day. It's easier to motivate yourself when you're not dragged down by mental clutter or tasks that you really don't enjoy but really need to do. You'll also be under less pressure as a result of your mental clutter and your lack of motivation associated with it.

A good way to approach this method is to start the day with a 'what is the frog?' mentality. Sit down and work out what the frog is. Once you know what it is, you can tackle it.

Do it, get it out of the way, rip off the Band-Aid, whatever term you want to use to describe it, just get it done and then look forward to the rest of the day and focus on the more enjoyable tasks you have.

You'll feel that familiar surge of motivation and optimism because the frog has been eaten, so to speak. You don't have to face it anymore, it's finished for that day at least, and you're free to focus on other things.

Try it and see what happens to your motivation and indeed, your mood.

Avoid Overthinking

Number one mood killer, number one procrastination killer, number one motivation killer and everything else to do with trying to get things done, is overthinking.

When you overthink you create problems that were never there in the first place. You focus on things that aren't happening, may never happen, and even if they do happen, they will probably be nowhere near as bad as you think. As a result, you stress yourself out, you become anxious, you block your own motivation and nothing gets done.

What does this do? Yes, it blocks you even more!

Overthinking creates a vicious cycle of negativity and also basically knocks your motivation out of the park and into a very large hole quite a long way away.

So, how can you stop yourself from overthinking, and why do you overthink in the first place?

We could write an entire book about this because it's such a huge subject, however, overthinking has its roots firmly in fear. It's not possible to be motivated when you're fearful, at least not motivated in a healthy way. Sure, you might be motivated to not do something, e.g. to avoid something happening, but that means you're motivating yourself to avoid something you fear, and when we talk more about fear you'll come to learn that they mean nothing anyway. So really, you're motivating yourself to do nothing and achieve nothing.

There are far more beneficial reasons to motivate yourself and ways to do it!

So, we overthink because we're scared of something. It's also very easy to start overthinking if you're someone who is generally quite anxious, but even the anxiety has its same roots in fear too.

You're worried about something, so you start to invent ways to prevent it from happening in your own mind. For instance, you might be scared of losing your job. There is probably no reason for you to lose your job and no real likelihood of it happening, but you're scared of the possibility because you know if it was to happen, you would struggle to make ends meet. This would then cause you a whole host of other problems.

Can you see how overthinking works? You start with one idea and it quickly snowballs into several other linked ideas. So in this case, you think 'oh it would be bad if I was to lose my job one day', and then you start to think of the reasons why it would be bad, e.g. you can't pay your rent, then that idea links into something else, such as I would end up having tome back in with my parents, what would people think of me. Then you start to imagine your friends judging you silently. As you can see, one small thought suddenly kicks off an avalanche of worries and fears that are not even likely to ever happen.

Overthinking is the world's biggest happiness killer and one of the most useless ways to spend your time. Despite that, many of us spend a lot of our time indulging in it.

Fear makes you negative when you're negative you're prone to anxiety and overthinking, and when you do that, your motivation isn't exactly high.

So, how can you stop yourself from overthinking?

You need to be aware of what you're doing and when. This means being mindful of your thoughts and acknowledging honestly when you're starting to turn molehills into mountains, overthinking small details.

Once you've realised that you're starting to overthink, try and change your focus. Don't focus on the negative things that might happen, focus on the positive things. Flip things around and look for the opportunities in a situation and not the things which would cause you to be unhappy and ruin your life. It does become easier over time, but this type of mental reframing also takes a little while to get used to and turn it into a habit.

Distraction is also a very useful way to stop yourself from overthinking. Try this:

- When you realise that you're starting to overthink something, tell yourself that you're overthinking, say it aloud or in your mind, whatever works for you
- Then, firmly say the word "stop" and push your hand out in a way to literally stop something. Again, it's best to do this aloud if you can, but

there might be situations when you can't do this, so in your own mind will still work well
- Then, when you've been firm enough to pause your thinking, quickly think of something else, something positive and something which will distract you
- Hold that distraction in your mind and don't allow the intrusive overthinking to comeback. After a few minutes, you'll find that it naturally abates and you're free of the thought that was starting to snowball

If you find that overthinking is becoming a chronic problem, e.g. it's something you're struggling with all the time, you might need to do some deep thinking and try and get to the roof of what is causing it. Are you always trying to look for perfection? Realise that perfection doesn't even exist and that as long as you're doing your best, that's enough.

You should also reassure yourself that whatever comes your way in life, you'll handle as best you can because that's what you've been doing up until this point in your life! You can't predict what is going to happen, and worrying about it isn't going to make it happen or stop it from happening. It's a huge waste of time, effort, happiness, and of course, motivation.

As you can see, there are a few different ways you can try and stop yourself from overthinking but the longer you've been doing this for, the longer it's going to take to try and stop this annoying habit from taking over your life. Stick with it, however, as it will be something you're glad you did and it will help you to become a more positive person in general.

When you allow overthinking to control you, you're also allowing fear to control you. By changing your mindset and unpicking fears, you'll realise that they 're not nearly as bad as you thought they would be, and they're also literally all in your head.

When you do this, you naturally become a more positive person and we've already established that when you're positive and confident, motivation quickly follows on.

Start slowly and try and banish one set of overthinking per day for the first week, increasing it to two for a few days, and then three etc. The more you do it, the more effective it will become.

Identify Your Personal Mental Blocks And Overcome Them

We all have personal triggers in many different situations in our lives.

We have anxiety triggers, jealousy triggers, emotional triggers in general, hunger triggers, anger triggers, you name it, you're bound to have some kind of trigger for it. So, what are your lack of motivation triggers? And, what are your motivation triggers?

Identifying both sets will allow you to minimise the negative ones and increase the positive ones.

Not sure how to begin? Keep a motivation diary. A little earlier we talked about keeping a diary to try and identify your most productive and therefore most motivated time of day, but within that, you could increase the amount of information you record and also write down the things you were doing or the things you were thinking which proceeded a boost or a dip in your motivation levels.

The 'Eat The Frog' method we talked about a little while ago is probably one of your lack of motivation triggers. Having a task to do which you don't really enjoy is enough to trigger a dip in motivation for anyone, but is there one specific task which this always occurs with?

For instance, do you hate taking the car for a service? Do you hate having to take minutes in a meeting? Which task really hits your 'frog' levels?

Knowing this task and your specific lack of motivation trigger, in this case, can help you to prepare for it. There's no getting out of doing it, most probably, but you can prepare yourself.

Whilst it's important to be aware of your lack of motivation triggers, it's perhaps more important to be aware of your motivation triggers, so you can expose yourself to more of them. Everyone has different personal triggers, so whilst when trying to figure out what yours are you might be tempted to ask a friend about theirs, you should realise that yours are likely to be subtly different, if not totally different.

Try the motivation diary method and see what elements of your life actually force you to feel more motivated without really trying. It might be the feeling of getting something done that motivates you, in which case that's a great motivator! It might be being prepared for meetings because you don't like the idea of not having all the information to hand. It might be that you like to have an easier day on a Friday, so you can wind down to the weekend. Whatever you find your motivation trigger to be, try and increase your exposure to it and use it to your benefit.

However, do be sure that your motivation trigger is a healthy one! We mentioned earlier in the book about positive motivation and negative motivation. Not all motivation is actually good. Knowing that you're being motivated by something healthy and useful will ensure that you remain upbeat and positive whilst you're still being productive, via your motivation method.

So, what about mental blocks? This is likely to go back to the frog in the room we mentioned earlier. For most people, having to do a task that they don't like doing is a huge mental block and a huge motivation blocker at the same time. However, you might have another mental block, perhaps a fear of speaking in public which causes you to avoid presentations, even though you need to start preparing for a big one you've got coming up next week.

A mental block, as with overthinking, has its roots in fear. When you have a mental block something is stopping you from focusing on it and probably making you avoid it. This means you have zero motivation in order to achieve it, and no desire to start. Or, maybe you have a desire to start in some way, because you want it to be done and over with, but the entire thing seems too big or too scary, so you procrastinate and don't do it at all.

The best way to focus on a mental block and banish it is to try and work out what you need to do, break it down into milestones, work towards the smaller tasks that make up the whole, and then celebrate every success as it comes your way. By doing this, you're making progress, but more importantly, you're showing yourself that there is nothing to fear and there is nothing to avoid.

The more you do this, the less power the block has on you.

So, spend some time thinking carefully about the things which you don't like to do, and the things which stop you from getting on with your day. The journal we mentioned earlier is a great way to show this information in pattern form, and you'll also be able to see clearly how often this particular block or trigger is a problem for you.

Knowledge is power, and once you know what you're facing, you can work to reduce its power and overcome it.

Have a Quick Workout

Health and wellbeing should always be at the forefront of your mind and one of the most important things in your life. Without your health, you literally have zero.

It's also very true to say that your health and wellbeing have a direct impact on your motivation levels.

When you're tired, when you're feeling under the weather or when you're suffering from symptoms of an illness, motivation is going to be hard to come by. That means placing importance on sleep, diet, and of course, exercise.

This particular method is going to talk more about how exercise is a vital tool in terms of boosting your motivation and getting more done. If you want to give yourself a quick boost, perhaps because you've found yourself in the middle of and focus slump mid-afternoon, a quick workout of some kind could be enough to get the blood flowing, increase oxygen moving up to and around the brain, and therefore kickstart those feel-good hormones. As a result, your motivation will return.

When we say 'have a quick workout' we don't necessarily mean head down to the local gym and get a sweat on, although if you want to do that, you'll certainly see benefits coming your way. This is also the case if you make those workouts a regular part of your weekly routine.

Any type of exercise will have the same effect, even going for a brisk walk outside. The fact that your heart is pumping that little bit faster means that oxygen and nutrients are making their way up to your brain, your brain is recognising these effects and the exercise is also triggering the release of endorphins, which raise your mood and help you feel good about the exercise you're doing.

All of this boosts your positivity, your confidence, and your focus. It's impossible for motivation not to be on the rise after all that!

You might not have time to do much in the way of exercise because you're at work or you have a lot to do, but a quick workout, literally five to ten minutes is all you need. Go for a walk, go for a run, do a few laps of the living room, jump on your exercise bike, run up and down the stairs - it can be anything!

Of course, incorporating exercise into your routine generally will help these effects become more commonplace and therefore reduce the number of times you need to manually boost your motivation because you've experienced a slump or a dip. Exercise benefits your general health and wellbeing, as well as your mental health, so you're getting serious benefits on many different fronts.

Perhaps the most motivating type of exercise is if you can join a team sport, or maybe even go to your local leisure centre and take part in a group exercise session. When other people are relying upon you, e.g. if you're playing as part of a team, you're more likely to go, you'll enjoy the social aspect of it, and you'll find that your motivation to help the team do well is sky-high. This motivation will then move out towards other areas of your life.

If you take part in a group exercise class, nobody is relying upon you, but you will find that your competitive spirit kicks in. You don't want to be the one at the back who can't keep up or the one who misses classes and sometimes attends, and sometimes doesn't. You want to be part of the gang, you want to be with the 'in' crowd. That in itself is a motivator not only to attend the class and focus on your fitness but as with the team sports example we just gave, that motivation will extend to other areas of your life.

Motivation is like a muscle. The more you flex it, the more easily you can call upon it when you need it, and the more ever-present it will be in your life generally.

So, it's time to make exercise a priority in your life, regardless of what type of exercise you choose to do.

Bribe Yourself With a Contract

A little earlier we talked about delayed gratification and how bribing yourself to continue, in order to receive a reward, can sometimes be the thing you need to get you over the line towards completing a difficult task. Now we're going to talk about another technique which, whilst similar in some ways, does have a few subtle differences and can be used in different situations.

Bribing yourself with a contract sounds quite negative, but when you break it down it's not at all negative and extremely positive in terms of the results you'll gain. This method is ideal for large tasks, those goals that you want to achieve but you know are going to take you a while to get there. We all know that when something takes a while, we often lose interest; we like to receive our results quickly and easily, we're inpatient by nature! So, when you hit that point where you're about to give up, simply because the results you want aren't coming fast enough, you can down tools for a second and do a little self-negotiation.

Tell yourself, 'if I complete x, y and z before the end of next week, I will reward myself with ... ' and insert something that you really want.

Whilst delayed gratification is for small things, e.g. if you finish a report by the end of the day you will buy yourself a chocolate bar on the way home, the contract idea covers more tasks to complete a sequence and a larger milestone and as a result, the reward has to be a little bigger in order to reflect the amount of motivation you need to trigger.

As you can see, it's similar, but it's different too.

The contract needs to cover specific actions and they need to work up towards a larger goal. For instance, if you're saving up for the deposit on a house and you have a plan that you want to have saved up your deposit by the end of the year, sit down and look at your progress so far. Do some maths - half the amount and half the time, so you want to have raised half the target amount within six months. Half that again so you're at the three-month mark, and then quarter it, so you need to raise a quarter of your target amount within three months. That covers three paydays at work.

Your contract to yourself here will be that if you save x amount every month for the next three months, without using it, dibbing into it, or borrowing it, you will go away for the weekend at the end of those three months.

That gives you something to work for, something to really aim towards and motivate you to do it, and you'll think twice about dibbing into those savings because you want that weekend away so badly.

You can use this method with any type of task, but it typically needs to cover a series of actions over a longer period of time. The point is that these larger tasks often require more motivation and have more chances of you throwing in the towel. The contract you make with yourself is something you adhere to in order to get the end result and in order to receive the reward. However, as with any type of contract, it is legally binding! This means that if you detour away from the terms and conditions you set out at the beginning, the reward doesn't come your way and you start from day 1 once more.

Is bribing yourself in this way ethical? That really depends on what you think about the situation, but you're not bribing anyone else, so if it works for you, that's perfectly fine!

Motivation can sometimes come from strange places, but our brains have a very solid reward centre, and by tapping into that, you can encourage the motivation to flow far more easily as a result.

Remember, however, no cheating!

Points to Remember From This Chapter

Throughout this chapter, we have talked about 15 different motivation techniques you can use to try and boost your motivation or magic it out of thin air. Some are overlapped with time management techniques, whilst others are standalone options you can use whenever you feel the need to boost your motivation.

It's really about finding a method that works for you and you may find that different situations require different approaches. You might even have different methods running side by side for different tasks. For instance, you use the contract method for a large goal you're trying to reach, but you might use the 'Eat The Frog' method during your working days, to get those tasks that cause you so much of a problem out of the way.

Try each one out and see which is best for you.

The main points to take from this very long chapter are:

- Learning how to boost motivation takes times, and not every method may work well for you
- Different methods might be useful for different situations, so it's perfectly okay to use different methods according to the situation you find yourself in
- It's a good idea to try each method out for yourself and separate the ones you like versus the ones that just don't work for you
- Motivation may ebb and flow throughout the course of one long task or aim, but staying on track means understanding when these occurrences are happening and working to boost your motivation back up again.

Conclusion

And there we have it! By this point, you should be feeling much more motivated than you were at the start!

Motivation is a subject which many people struggle with, simply because it's not something you can see or touch with your hands. You can feel it, however, and when you're brimming with plenty of the big M, the effects are very clear to see too.

There are countless different things that can affect how motivated you are, and you might find yourself motivated in one area of your life, and sadly lacking in motivation in another. For instance, you might be full of ideas and motivation to redecorate your house, but when it comes to a task at work, you might be struggling in all different kinds of ways.

This is normal, and if you're finding yourself in these types of situations, you can take heart in the fact that you're no different from anyone else! There is nobody on this planet who is 100% motivated,

100% of the time, in every single area of their lives. It's simply not possible to be that driven all the time. We all have our off days, and those are the days when you need to recognise that your mind and body need a rest, and then put into place a little self-care.

The need for self-care is something that many people overlook or don't take seriously. Thankfully, these days we're all becoming a little more aware of the importance of ensuring good mental health and giving it as much air time as our physical health. When your mind is tired, you need a little TLC and you're struggling to focus, you're not going to find motivation comes to you very easily at all. In some cases, it may not come, no matter how hard you try. This is a sign that you need to rest, look after yourself, take some downtime, and then regroup and try again. You'll more than likely find that after this period of self-care your motivation is back up and running, and probably better than ever before.

Where to Begin

We've covered a lot of information, so you might be wondering where you're supposed to begin in boosting your motivation levels. There is no right or wrong answer, but it's a good idea to start identifying your trouble spots.

Are there specific tasks at work that cause you to want to procrastinate? How about in your personal life? What areas do you lack motivation in, and can you pinpoint why?

The more information you have, the easier it will be in terms of figuring out where your starting point should be. It might also be that you really don't have a huge problem with motivation and that you simply want to know a few easy ways you can boost your motivation when it's starting to run on empty a little.

It happens to the best of us from time to time, and even the most motivated people on the planet struggle occasionally. In that case, you simply need to try out the different strategies we've covered throughout the book and identify the ones which work best for you. From there, you can adopt them at the necessary times in your life.

If you're finding that motivation is a huge problem for you, that you struggle to summon up the energy and the focus to really get started on anything or keep going, that could be a sign of a bigger problem that needs addressing, but the good news is that nothing is unsurmountable.

If this is your situation, do you feel happy in your job? Are there specific areas in your personal life that are causing you to have one huge mental block?

Do a little soul searching and really work out where your problems might lie. It will be difficult at first and you might unearth some things you didn't really want to focus on, but denying there is an issue isn't going to help you become more motivated. Facing problems head-on shows courage, but it also shows that you're keen and willing to kick start your motivation issue and overcome problems.

That, ladies and gentlemen, is bravery.

Motivation can become your best friend if you allow it to be. Motivation will push you to achieve more than you ever dreamed of, and it will allow you to make huge leaps forward when you probably struggled to even take a step before. All you need to do is encourage it and create a foundation on which it can build and grow. Now you're more aware of what motivation is and what you need in order to build that foundation, you'll find it far easier to encourage more of it into your life.

This can be the motivation to tick items off your daily to-do list, it can be the motivation to take baby steps towards a huge, life-changing goal, or it can be the motivation to simply take control of your day, enabling you to be the one in control.

Whatever it is, and whatever you need motivation for, learning how to encourage its growth will benefit you in terms of health, wellbeing, confidence, productivity, positivity, and beyond.

All that is left to say now is good luck. Dedicate yourself to using the methods we've covered in this book and be brave enough to face any problems that are causing you to experience a direct motivation block. Declutter your life, declutter your mind, ready to make room for all the wonderful experiences and situations you're going to invite into your life as a result of your hard work and effort.

A Short message from the Author:

Hey, are you enjoying the book? I'd love to hear your thoughts!

Many readers do not know how hard reviews are to come by, and how much they help an author. Reviews alone are what typically makes my book stand out in the crowd, persuades another person to choose this book.

I would be incredibly thankful if you could take just

60 seconds is all it takes to write a brief review - even if it's just a few sentences - on Amazon, Audible, Goodreads, or whatever bookstore you purchased this book from!

Thank you for taking the time to share your thoughts!

More from Jean-Claude Leveque

-Conquer your Emotions
-Conquer your Concentration
-Conquer your Purpose
-F*ck Anxiety
-F*ck Panic Attacks

www.ingramcontent.com/pod-product-compliance
Lightning Source LLC
Chambersburg PA
CBHW021437080526
44588CB00009B/569